正誤表

p.49
English Composition 2. 誤>(look more closel を使って)　正>(look more closely を使って)

p.87
【Reading Comprehension Questions 解答】誤>7.T　正>7.F

p.98
【English Composition 解答】
誤>He liked to have students watch campaign advertisements to look for their tools of persuasion.
正>They mainly focused on topics that were concerning at the time such as wars,

p.101
【English Composition 解答】
誤>1. Meg Grigal works with an organization called Think College.
　2. There is a campaign to encourage young people with mental disabilities to consider college.
　3. VCU discovered one student who had no idea how artistic he was.
正>1. Recently, VOA reported on the importance of counties in the United States.
　2. There are more than 3,000 counties nationwide.
　3. The Census Bureau reports that 1,653 counties lost population between 2010 and 2015.

語学シリーズ
第❹巻

ボイス・オブ・アメリカ（VOA）
ニュースで学ぶ英語 レベル2

杉田米行　監修

佐藤晶子・山西敏博・竹林修一・奈須　健　著

大学教育出版

はじめに

　ボイス・オブ・アメリカ（Voice of America: VOA）はアメリカ合衆国連邦政府運営の国営放送で，毎日ニュースを配信しています．本書は，パブリックドメイン *VOA Learning English: We are American English* で取り上げられたニュースを中心に，14 カテゴリーの記事に取り組み，終了時にはアメリカの概略を把握するとともに TOEIC, TOEFL の出題形式に合わせた復習問題を解くことによって，実践的英語力の習得を目指します．

　読解のための語彙，文法および構文ノートは予習時の便宜を考え，ページの許す限り，できるだけ詳しくつけるようにしました．ただし，最初からノートに頼るのではなく，まず自分で辞書や参考書に当たることが大切です．

　ノートを付記するに際して，多くのリソースのお世話になりました．詳細を挙げることはできませんが，この場をお借りして感謝の意を評させていただきます．

　大阪大学杉田米行教授からは，本書を完成させるうえで貴重な助言をいただきました．代表取締役社長佐藤守氏には企画段階から大変お世話になりました．ここに心からお礼もうしあげます．

平成 29 年 1 月 1 日

著　者

本書の使い方

『ボイス・オブ・アメリカ（VOA）ニュースで学ぶ英語　レベル2』は自分で学習できるように工夫しています．記事のリスニング教材は *VOA Learning English*（http://learningenglish.voanews.com/）のサイトでダウンロードできます．URLを載せてあります．そこにアクセスしてください．iPhoneやandroidスマートフォンでアクセスできます．

記事をウェブサイト上で読みたい場合は，Googleなどの検索サイトで"voa"と課題文のタイトルを打ち込んで検索してください．（例「voa You Do the Math」と打ち込むと，検索サイトでタイトルが出てきます．そのタイトルをクリックすると，課題文にアクセスすることができます．）スピーカーのマークをクリックすると英語の音声が流れてきます．

テキストのリーディング，リスニング課題の（　　）内の数字は音声の経過時間です．予習復習の際に利用してください．Listening Comprehensionは30～40秒，リーディングの課題箇所の時間は5分以内です．合計6分もあれば十分に聴き取れます．

VOA Learning English の教材はLevel 1，Level 2，Level 3があります．本書はほとんどがLevel 2の教材で構成されています．Listening Comprehensionは，動詞を聞き取ることに重点を置きました．English Compositionも動詞を使いこなすことに重点を置いて出題しています．文章の先頭にある主語を聞き取り，肝心の内容を決定する動詞が聞き取ることができるよう練習してください．

本書は150ワード／分レベルの英語を聞き取ることで，英語に慣れ，理解を深めることを目指します．さらに上級を目指す人はLevel 3やVOA（http://www.voanews.com/）のウェブサイトにアクセスしてください．

本書のUnit14の後に新形式問題に対応したミニTOEICテスト2回分を掲載しています．テスト1は17題，テスト2は20題の問題数です．復習テストとして利用してください．音源は大学教育出版のホームページの書籍サポートメニューからダウンロードできます．（http://www.kyoiku.co.jp）

ボイス・オブ・アメリカ（VOA）ニュースで学ぶ英語　レベル2

目　次

はじめに……………………………………………………………………… *i*
本書の使い方………………………………………………………………… *ii*

Unit 1. Science and Technology
Truck Completes First Driverless Shipment: Beer …………………… *1*

Unit 2. Gender
Flashback: The Fight for Women's Right to Vote ……………………… *6*

Unit 3. Education
You Do the Math …………………………………………………………… *11*

Unit 4. Environmental Protection
Oceans To Hold More Plastic Than Fish by 2050 ……………………… *16*

Unit 5. US Political History
George Washington: President, Man, Myth ……………………………… *21*

Unit 6. Sports
Chicago Cubs Win World Series …………………………………………… *26*

Unit 7. Public Welfare
Program Helps Lift American Families Out of Poverty ……………… *31*

Unit 8. Agriculture
Robot Can Help With Farm Work ………………………………………… *36*

Unit 9. Politics
2016 US Election is Hard for Civics Teachers…………………………… *41*

Unit 10. Culture
Hold The Butter! Modern Diets Meet Holiday Traditions ……………… *46*

Unit 11. Public Health and Social Security
      One-Third of U.S. Counties Have More Deaths than Births *51*

Unit 12. Racial and Ethnic Issue
      Should Offensive Place Names Be Changed? *56*

Unit 13. Religion
      One in Four Married Americans Do Not Share Same Religion as Wife, Husband *61*

Unit 14. US Pop Culture
      Winans: Music, God and Family *67*

復習用　ミニ TOEIC テスト 2 回分 *72*
訳例と解答...*84*
付録　お役立ちサイト *134*
参考文献...*136*

Unit 1

Science and Technology

Truck Completes First Driverless Shipment: Beer

http://learningenglish.voanews.com/a/self-driving-truck-completes-worlds-first-driverless-shipment-with-load-of-budweiser-beer/3568688.html

出典：Public domain Pixabay under Creative Commons CC0

00:00-04:15

1   A self-driving truck has completed a delivery of goods for a company for the first time.

 The truck recently transported a full load of Budweiser beer in the western state of Colorado. The vehicle drove without the assistance of a driver for most of the 190-kilometer trip without problems.

 Otto, a company owned by the ride-sharing business Uber, operated the driverless truck.

High-tech beer run

 The truck carried about 50,000 cans of beer from the city of Fort Collins to Colorado Springs. During that time, the vehicle kept an average speed of about 89 kilometers per hour during the two-hour trip, Otto said.

 The company said a trained driver was inside the truck for the entire trip. But he only sat in front and drove the truck as it was entering and leaving the interstate highway. The rest of the time, he sat in a part of the truck used for relaxing and sleeping.

Not for city driving

Otto's autonomous technology is designed for use only on highways. These wide roads do not have traffic stops or people crossing the road. The technology, including parts and software, can be added to existing trucks for about $30,000.

Otto's co-founder is Anthony Levandowski, a former self-driving car engineer for Google. He said he thinks the most important thing computers will do over the next ten years is drive cars and trucks for people.

He added that his company is very concerned about safety. He said people should not be afraid to share the roads with Otto's driverless trucks.

"It's like a train on software rails," he explains. "When you see a vehicle driving with nobody in it, you will know that it's very unlikely to get into a collision."

Anheuser-Busch said the driverless delivery showed how the technology is becoming the next great innovation in transportation. The company plans to use self-driving trucks to help move more than 1.2 million beer loads each year.

But the company says it will still need people in the driverless future. Humans will be used to do limited driving, oversee the loading process and manage trips.

I'm Bryan Lynn.

Bryan Lynn wrote this story for VOA Learning English, based on reports from Reuters and the Associated Press. Mario Ritter was the editor.

We want to hear from you. Write to us in the Comments section, and visit our Facebook page.

読解のための語彙，文法および構文

p.1 ℓ.1	a self-driving truck: 自動で運転をするトラック
p.1 ℓ.1	a delivery of goods: 商品輸送
p.1 ℓ.4	vehicle: 車
p.1 ℓ.6	the ride-sharing business: 運転を共有する事業
p.1 ℓ.8	run: 経営　「走らせる」という意味合いから「(企業の) 経営」という意味をなす
p.1 ℓ.12	a trained driver: 熟練の運転手　「訓練がなされた」という意味合いから
p.1 ℓ.17	autonomous technology: 自動運転技術
p.1 ℓ.18	traffic stops: 信号機

p.2 ℓ.20　co-founder: 共に創業した者

p.2 ℓ.20　found-founded- founded:「創業する」
　　　　＊find-found-found:「見つける」と類似しているので注意

p.2 ℓ.21　computer 〜 years の文が挿入節となって the most important thing を修飾し，そこから is が動詞となり，最後に（to）drive の目的語につながる

p.2 ℓ.23　is concerned about: 〜に対して注意を払う

p.2 ℓ.24　driverless truck: 無人（運転手のいない）トラック

p.2 ℓ.26　be unlikely to: 〜しそうにない

p.2 ℓ.26　get into a collision: 衝突する

p.2 ℓ.28　the driverless delivery showed 〜: 無生物主語になっていることから，訳出する時にはこれを副詞的に捉えると，意味がとりやすい

p.2 ℓ.29　innovation: 革新

p.2 ℓ.32　oversee: 監視する

p.2 ℓ.32　the loading process: 積荷の過程

p.2 ℓ.35　editor: 編集者

Reading Comprehension Questions

次の各文が，本文の内容に合っていればTを，合っていない場合はFを，括弧内に記入してください．

1. (　) This is the second time that a self-driving truck delivered products for a company.
2. (　) The vehicle shipped a lot of beer in the eastern state of Colorado.
3. (　) The truck could move without any driver's support for about 200-kilometer travel.
4. (　) Mr. Uber ran an office which shared car-sharing business Otto
5. (　) The truck owned by Otto shipped around half of a hundred thousand cans of beer from the city of Fort Collins to Colorado Springs.
6. (　) Otto mentioned the truck kept moving around 180 kilometers.
7. (　) No driver was inside the vehicle except for a veteran driver while the car was running for the travel.
8. (　) The driver kept on sitting and driving all the time, including entering and leaving the interstate highway.
9. (　) The trained driver was seated in a part of the truck which was used

for feeling relaxed and falling asleep all the time.
10. (　) Otto designed driverless technology on every road.

Listening Comprehension Questions

次の英語を聴いて空欄を埋めてください．

http://learningenglish.voanews.com/audio/audio/298267.html

(00:02-00:28)

Hello, listeners. My name is Bryan Lynn. Today, I'm going to talk about driverless (　　　). The company Otto had a design of autonomous (　　　). This is used only on (　　　), because the truck without driving (　　　) can move without taking care of traffic (　　　) or pedestrians. In (　　　), we can add the technology, including parts and software, to the (　　　) trucks with $30,000.

English Composition

次の日本文を英文に直してください．

1. 政府が次の10年に向けて行わなければならない最も重要な行動は，経済活動の復興である．（government, revive economic action を用いて）

2. 彼女の経営する食品会社は，食の安全に対して長年細心の注意を払ってきているということを，彼女は付け加えた．（food company, be concerned about, meals を用いて）

3. オートバイによる配達をすることで，都心部における交通渋滞の中で，二輪車がいかに輸送に対してすばらしい革新となっているか，といったことが示されている．（motorcycle, show, traffic jam, urban place を用いて）

ひとくちコラム

「Uber」について，リサイクル可能な衣類を回収して東北に届けるというチャリティーイベント「Uber RECYCLE」が，2015年10月4日に開催された．「Uber RECYCLE」とは，そのイベントが開催されている期間の中で，対象エリア内でウーバーのアプリケーションを開くと，配車を行うのと共に「RECYCLE」メニューが現れ，前の日に講習を受講した，一般のボランティア運転手が自らの車を運転しながら衣類を回収するという催し物であった．さらに，2015年10月20日，国家戦略特区諮問会議の中で，安倍晋三首相は「過疎地などで観光客の交通手段として，自家用自動車の活用を拡大する」という答弁を行い，地方に住む一般の者が自らの車を用いて有料で送迎を行う「ライドシェア（相乗り）」を可能にする規制緩和を検討するよう指示を行った．その後，2016年5月には，トヨタ自動車とライドシェア領域における協業を検討する旨の覚書を締結した．加えて，2016年5月26日には京丹後市のNPO法人がUberの仕組みを採用して，一般の人々による有償旅客輸送を開始した．このように，Uberは徐々に日本国内にも浸透しつつある．

Unit 2

Gender

Flashback: The Fight for Women's Right to Vote

http://learningenglish.voanews.com/a/women-voting-flashback-woman-suffrage/3585206.html

Flashback: The Fight for Women's Right to Vote
出典：VOA, Public Domain
http://gdb.voanews.com/ 2c592e6c-1450-4620-b994-71aa55684006.jpg

00:00-03:18

1　　The year is 1913. A new president has been elected and is about to take office. But when he arrives at the train station in Washington, DC, few people are there to meet him.

"Where are the crowds?" he asks.

5　　They are already on Pennsylvania Avenue, watching something the American public has never seen before: thousands of women, marching in the streets.

What do they want? The right to vote.

"The U.S. Constitution didn't say one thing about who could vote in its initial form. All of the power over who could vote was left to the states."

10　　Robyn Muncy is a history professor at the University of Maryland, College Park.

She explains that in America's political system, power is divided between the federal government and the states.

"That meant that suffragists in the late 19th century had a choice: They could 15 either try to get a federal amendment … or, they could work state by state, where in a lot of cases, women had a lot more power at the state level."

Women decided to do both. The struggle for woman suffrage took place at the federal and state level from the 19th century through the 20th. "Suffrage" means the right to vote.

The 19th century: grassroots campaigns in the states

At first, only a few women were asking for suffrage. They said women had the same value as men, so they should have the same political and legal rights, too.

These women traveled across the U.S., giving talks about equal rights and meeting with lawmakers in town after town.

But Jean Baker, a historian from Goucher College in Maryland, says their ideas were not always popular.

"There are stories of the women being chased after they finished their lecture, and they might be going back to a home to spend the night. And people would be peppering them with all kinds of rotten eggs, et cetera, et cetera.

"But they also suffered from the opposition of the majority opinion."

At the time, most people – including women – thought that women voting just wasn't natural. They believed that men and women were fundamentally opposites.

"That men were competitive, they were aggressive by nature, they were self-assertive by nature. And they belonged – they were fitted – for public life.

"While women were by nature nurturing, cooperative and thrived really within the confines of their own homes."

Historian Robyn Muncy says that, nevertheless, suffragists operated grassroots campaigns across the U.S. They worked town by town, persuading their neighbors, persuading people in their churches, and then trying to persuade their state legislators to enfranchise women.

■ 読解のための語彙，文法および構文

- *p.6 ℓ.1* is about to: まさに～しようとする
- *p.6 ℓ.1* take office: 着任する
- *p.6 ℓ.5* watching something the American public has never seen before: something を the American public 以下が説明している．
- *p.6 ℓ.7* right: 権利
- *p.6 ℓ.8* Constitution: 憲法
- *p.6 ℓ.9* initial form: 前文
- *p.6 ℓ.9* be left to the states: 原義は「州に取り残される」より，意訳で「アメリカに居

住することができる」となる．

p.6 ℓ.13	federal government: 連邦政府	
p.6 ℓ.14	suffragist: 婦人参政権論者	
p.6 ℓ.14	choice: 選択，ここでは「参政権」の意味	
p.6 ℓ.15	federal amendment: 連邦法案の改正	
p.6 ℓ.16	power: 力，ここでは「権限」の意味	
p.7 ℓ.17	struggle: 闘争	
p.7 ℓ.17	woman suffrage: 婦人参政権	
p.7 ℓ.22	legal right: 立法的な権利	
p.7 ℓ.24	meeting with: ～と会合をする	
p.7 ℓ.24	lawmaker: 法案作成者	
p.7 ℓ.29	pepper A with B: A に B を投げつける	
p.7 ℓ.29	et cetera: ～など（フランス語） etc. と略される． ＝ and so on	
p.7 ℓ.30	suffer from: ～で苦しむ	
p.7 ℓ.30	opposition: 反対	
p.7 ℓ.30	majority opinion: 多数派意見	
p.7 ℓ.33	competitive: 競争心が強い	
p.7 ℓ.33	aggressive: 高圧的な	
p.7 ℓ.33	by nature: 生まれつき	
p.7 ℓ.33	self-assertive: 自己主張が強い	
p.7 ℓ.35	nurturing: 大切に育てる，ここでは「おしとやかにする」の意味	
p.7 ℓ.35	cooperative: 協調性がある	
p.7 ℓ.35	thrive: 繁栄する	
p.7 ℓ.36	confine: とどめる，ここでは「家に閉じこもる」の意味	
p.7 ℓ.37	grassroot: 草の根	
p.7 ℓ.38	persuade: 説得する	
p.7 ℓ.39	state legislator: 州の代表議員	
p.7 ℓ.40	enfranchise: 参政権を与える	

Reading Comprehension Questions

次の各文が，本文の内容に合っていればTを，合っていない場合はFを，括弧内に記入してください．

1. (   ) A new president in the U.S. has been chosen and was on the point of taking up in the year of World War Ⅰ.

Unit 2 Flashback: The Fight for Women's Right to Vote 9

2. (　　) Quite a few people are at the station in order to welcome the new president.
3. (　　) So many females were marching on Pennsylvania Avenue and that scene was what the American public has not experienced before.
4. (　　) These women would like to have a choice to join an election.
5. (　　) The U.S. Constitution mentioned in its initial form that all men are created equal.
6. (　　) Authority is included either the federal government or the states in the political system in the U.S.
7. (　　) All females had a right to vote after 1850.
8. (　　) When a male has a right to vote, he is called a Suffragist.
9. (　　) Only a few females appealed that males had the same value as females, therefore, they should have the same political and legal rights as women, too.
10. (　　) These suffragists moved around the States and talked about equal rights and had several meeting with those who made laws in many places.

Listening Comprehension Questions

次の英語を聴いて空欄を埋めてください．

例）http://learningenglish.voanews.com/audio/audio/298267.html

(00:02-00:28)

Hello, I'm Robyn Muncy. I'm a professor of (　　　　) at the University of Maryland. Now, I'll mention the authority in the U.S. It is divided between the federal (　　　　) and the states in the U.S. political system. That meant that women (　　) wanted to have a right to vote in the late 19th century had a choice to join politics. In addition, (　　　) had much more authority at the state level. Around five out of one (　　　　) females wanted to have a choice for election in the early 19th.

English Composition

次の日本文を英文に直してください．

1. その高校には新しい校長が選ばれ，まさに着任しようとしていた．（principal, be about to, take office を用いて）

2. 多くの群集たちは多数派意見の反対に賛同していた．（crowds, agree with を用いて）

3. 女性は，生まれつきおしとやかに，協調性を持ち，家庭で穏やかにふるまっていることで大成をするものなのだ，と，かつては言われていた．（used to, 現在完了形を用いて）

ひとくちコラム

　教育は人権の中のひとつであり，すべての子どもは教育を受ける権利を与えられている．また，各国の政府は，すべての子どもたちが教育を受けることができることを保証する義務がある．しかしながら，一方では，世界各地で少女たちが学ぶことを続けようとすると，暴力に直面することが数多くある．

　戦争を行っている国々では，武装集団に捕らえられたり，通学中や学校自体が襲撃された時に死傷してしまったりする少女もいる．難民キャンプで生活をしている少女たちの中には，性的虐待や性的搾取の危険にさらされている者もいる．

　世界にはアムネスティという団体がある．この団体は，関連する全団体の協力の下において，政府関係者と学校を含む関係機関に対して，積極的に対策を講じるよう，に以下のような要求をしてきている．

　・少女に対するすべての形態の暴力を禁止すること
　・学校を安全にすること
　・少女に対する暴力事件に対応すること
　・被害を受けた少女に支援サービスを提供すること
　・少女が通学する際の障害（初等教育費など）を除去すること
　・少女を虐待から守ること

　パキスタン人のマララ・ユスフザイ氏は，中学時代に女子教育の充実を訴えて，銃弾に倒れながらも，その後18歳でノーベル平和賞を授与した．彼女もこうした上記の訴えを全面的に押し出している一人である．

Unit 3　　　　　　　　　　　　　　　　Education

You Do the Math

http://learningenglish.voanews.com/a/3549624.html You Do the Math

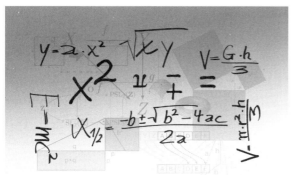

出典：Public domain Pixabay under Creative Commons CC0g

[00:00-03:38]

1　　Hello and welcome to Words and Their Stories from VOA Learning English.
　　On this program we explain how to use common expressions in American English. We also explore the origins of these expressions. Where *do* they come from?
5　　Today we are talking about expressions related to numbers. Why? Well, you do the math! VOA does a lot of programs, and sooner or later we were going to get to this one.
　　The verbal phrase "do the math" means to examine the facts and figures to reach a conclusion, especially when the answer is very clear.
10　　For example, let's say I love animals. I spend all my savings on caring for stray cats and dogs. When my friend asks why I never go on vacation, I can simply point to my seven cats and five dogs and say, "Money for vacations? You do the math!"
　　Of course, before children can do even basic math they must learn to count.

But counting numbers is not the only meaning of the word "count." Consider a famous quote by the scientist Albert Einstein. He reportedly said, "Not everything that counts can be counted. Not everything that can be counted counts."

This quote is a pun, a play on words. It plays with two meanings of the word "count." Count means to determine the total number of something. It also means to have value or importance. Things that matter, things that are important ... count.

Let's hear count used in a dialogue. These two friends are talking about an upcoming U.S. election. Take note that a third definition of "count" -- meaning "depend" -- is used.

A: Are you voting in November?
B: Why should I? My vote doesn't count.
A: What do you mean it doesn't count?! After they close the polls workers count all the votes!
A: What I mean is that voters in D.C. don't have representatives in Congress. So, even though my vote for president is officially counted, my opinion about what should happen in my own neighborhood doesn't count. And many people in D.C. are sick of it. You can count on that.
B: Oh, that's right. I didn't count that fact. I live in Maryland and have 10 representatives in Congress. So, my voice does count more than yours.
A: Hm-mm.

That is a lot of counting!

After counting, many children learn to solve simple addition problems. They learn that 1 + 1 = 2 and 2 + 2 = 4 and so on and so on.

読解のための語彙，文法および構文

p.11 ℓ.2	how to use: 使い方，使用法
p.11 ℓ.2	common expression: 慣用的な表現，よく使われる表現
p.11 ℓ.3	explore:（詳しく）〜を調査（探索）する
p.11 ℓ.3	come from: 〜から来る（伝来する），〜に由来する
p.11 ℓ.5	talk about: 〜について語る
p.11 ℓ.5	relate to: 〜に関連している，〜に関わる
p.11 ℓ.6	do the math: 計算する，自分で考える
p.11 ℓ.6	sooner or later: いつかは，遅かれ早かれ
p.11 ℓ.8	verbal phrase: 動詞句

p.11 ℓ.8	examine:	～を調査する，調べる，分析する
p.11 ℓ.8	facts and figures:	正確な情報
p.11 ℓ.10	for example:	例えば，例として
p.11 ℓ.10	let's say:	たとえば～したとすれば，仮に～したとして，～だと仮定して
p.11 ℓ.10	all one's savings:	～の貯金全て
p.11 ℓ.10	care for:	～を大事に思う，～のことを心配する
p.11 ℓ.11	stray cats and dogs:	野良猫・野良犬
p.11 ℓ.11	go on vacation:	休暇に出掛ける，休暇を取る
p.11 ℓ.12	point to:	～に注意を向ける，～を指摘する
p.11 ℓ.14	of course:	もちろん，確かに，言うまでもなく
p.11 ℓ.14	learn to:	～する方法を習得する，努力して～できるようになる
p.12 ℓ.16	quote:	引用，引用文，引用句
p.12 ℓ.16	"Not everything that counts can be counted":	大事なもの全てが数えられるわけではない
p.12 ℓ.17	"Not everything that can be counted counts":	数えられるもの全てが大事なわけではない
p.12 ℓ.18	pun:	駄洒落，語呂合わせ
p.12 ℓ.18	play on words:	言葉遊び，洒落，語呂合わせ
p.12 ℓ.18	play with:	～で遊ぶ，もてあそぶ
p.12 ℓ.19	total number:	総計，累計
p.12 ℓ.20	matter:	重要（問題）である，大きな違いがある
p.12 ℓ.21	dialogue:	対話，会話
p.12 ℓ.22	upcoming:	今度の，次回の，近づきつつある，もうすぐやってくる
p.12 ℓ.22	take note:	注意する，気づく
p.12 ℓ.22	third definition:	第3（3番目）の定義
p.12 ℓ.23	depend:	（～によって）決まる，左右される，当てにする，信頼する
p.12 ℓ.24	vote:	投票する
p.12 ℓ.25	count:	有効である
p.12 ℓ.26	polls:	投票所
p.12 ℓ.28	voter:	有権者
p.12 ℓ.28	D.C.:	ワシントン・コロンビア特別区
p.12 ℓ.28	representative:	代理人，代表者，下院議員
p.12 ℓ.28	Congress:	アメリカ連邦議会
p.12 ℓ.29	even though:	～であるけれども，～であるにしても，～にもかかわらず
p.12 ℓ.29	officially:	公式に，正式に

p.12 ℓ.30	what should happen:	何かあったこと，起こったこと
p.12 ℓ.30	neighborhood:	地区，地域，区域，近隣
p.12 ℓ.31	be sick of:	〜にうんざりしている
p.12 ℓ.31	count on:	〜を頼りにする，期待する，当てにする，予想する
p.12 ℓ.32	that's right:	その通りです，間違いありません，そういうことです
p.12 ℓ.36	addition problem:	付加，足し算の問題
p.12 ℓ.37	and so on:	〜など

Reading Comprehension Questions

次の各文が，本文の内容に合っていればTを，合っていない場合はFを，括弧内に記入してください．

1. (　) Doing analysis of the accurate information, we use the verbal phrase "do the math"
2. (　) Many animal protection activists care for poor creatures by choice.
3. (　) Before children learn how to count, they will study basic math.
4. (　) The word "count" carries a great deal of meaning.
5. (　) Albert Einstein, scientist, was also known as a poet.
6. (　) Albert Einstein made a famous quote about counting numbers.
7. (　) Many voters in D.C. have a high expectation for their representatives.
8. (　) Many voters in D.C. become bored with going to their polls, because they have to line up there early on the day.
9. (　) There are more than eight representatives in Maryland.
10. (　) As soon as a lot of children learn to count, they will try to solve some complex problems.

Listening Comprehension Questions

次の英語を聴いて空欄を埋めてください．

http://learningenglish.voanews.com/a/how-to-write-a-college-paper/3642289.html

`00:00-00:51`

Strong writing is one of the most (　) (　) for any college student. Many non-native English speakers (　) (　) (　) what professors in the U.S. expect from a college paper. A college paper is a piece of writing than can be (　) (　) (　) 20 or more pages. Even native English-speaking college students (　　) (　　) how to succeed with such a difficult responsibility.

English Composition

次の日本文を英文に直してください．

1. 数学の問題は，思ったほど難しくなかった．（as difficult as を使って）

2. 昨夜，宿題をやってしまっていたら良かったのに．（wish を使って）

3. 才能があっても，努力を怠れば失敗する可能性が高くなる．（even if を使って）

ひとくちコラム

　アメリカでは幸運を呼ぶラッキーナンバーとして，数字の『7』が挙げられる．これは，旧約聖書の中で，神が世界を作った時に6日働いて7日目に休んだという記述があることから，『7』は「世界」や「完全」を意味する神の数字でもあると考えられている．一方，「ラッキーセブン」という言葉の起源は諸説ある．過去にアメリカのメジャーリーグで優勝のかかった試合で，7回に平凡なフライを打ち上げた選手の打球が，強風にのってホームランになってしまったという奇跡的な出来事や，7回に比較的逆転劇が起きることが多いことなど野球にまつわる説が多い．そのため，勝負のターニングポイントとしても意識づけられるようになった．

Unit 4

Environmental Protection

Oceans To Hold More Plastic Than Fish by 2050

http://learningenglish.voanews.com/a/oceans-could-hold-more-plastics-than-fish-2050/3166848.html

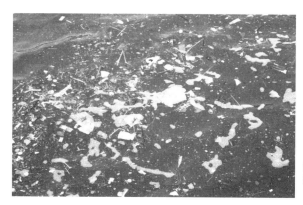

Oceans To Hold More Plastic Than Fish by 2050
出典：Public domain Pixabay under Creative Commons CC0

[00:00-03:35]

There will be more plastic than fish in the world's oceans by 2050 unless more recycling takes place. That is what a new report from the World Economic Forum and Ellen MacArthur Foundation warns.

If the current trend continues, the report said, oceans will contain one ton of plastic for every three tons of fish in 2025.

By 2050, plastics will weigh more than fish, the report said.

The problem is that each year at least 8 million tons of plastics end up in oceans around the world.

The report said this is the same as dumping the contents of one garbage truck into the ocean every minute.

Not all plastic ends up in the ocean because someone throws a plastic bottle into the water.

Plastic containers and other trash thrown onto streets and sidewalks often are swept into oceans. The debris travels from storm drains during rain storms, said the environmental group Marine Defenders.

Some end up in gyres. A gyre is a big whirlpool that traps and moves the plastic in circles.

Unlike other types of trash in the ocean, the plastic never bio-degrades. That means it does not break down.

There is a way to slow the amount of plastics going into the oceans -- people can recycle more. That is a major recommendation of the report by the World Economic Forum and Ellen MacArthur Foundation.

The report's authors say that currently only about 14 percent of plastics are recycled.

It said research in Europe shows as much as 53 percent of plastic could be recycled using available technology.

The report says that another solution is using less plastic for packaging products. But that is not likely to happen, the report's authors say.

"Given plastic packaging's many benefits, both the likelihood and desirability of an across-the-board drastic reduction in the volume of plastic packaging used is clearly low," the report said.

But the authors note reducing the use of plastics should be tried "where possible."

For decades, scientists warned that plastics are killing fish. The Natural Resources Defense Council said research shows that fish are dying from choking after eating plastics. Another cause of death is that plastics cause "intestinal blockage and starvation," the environmental group said.

I'm Mario Ritter.

読解のための語彙，文法および構文

p.16 ℓ.1	**unless:** ～でない限り，～である場合を除いて	
p.16 ℓ.2	**take place:** 行われる，開催される，起こる	
p.16 ℓ.2	**new report:** 最新の報告	
p.16 ℓ.2	**World Economic Forum:** 世界経済フォーラム，世界経済協議会（WEF）	
p.16 ℓ.3	**Ellen MacArthur Foundation:** エレン・マッカーサー財団	
p.16 ℓ.4	**current trend:** 現在（最近，最新）の傾向，動向	
p.16 ℓ.5	**every:** ～ごとに，～おきに，毎～	
p.16 ℓ.6	**weigh:** 重荷になる，重くのしかかる	
p.16 ℓ.7	**at least:** 少なくとも，低く見積もっても	

p.16 ℓ.7	end up in:	最後に〜に行く
p.16 ℓ.9	be the same as:	〜と同じである，〜も同然である
p.16 ℓ.9	dump:	（中身を）放出する，投げ捨てる
p.16 ℓ.9	content:	中身，内容，内容物
p.16 ℓ.9	garbage truck:	ごみ収集（運搬）車
p.16 ℓ.10	every minute:	ずっと，全工程
p.16 ℓ.11	not all:	全てが〜とは限らない（主に部分否定で用いる）
p.16 ℓ.13	container:	入れ物，容器，箱
p.16 ℓ.13	trash:	くず，ごみ，がらくた
p.16 ℓ.13	throw:	（物を）投げる
p.16 ℓ.13	streets and sidewalks:	車道と歩道
p.16 ℓ.14	sweep into:	〜の中にさっと入っていく
p.16 ℓ.14	debris:	（破壊された物の）破片，瓦礫
p.16 ℓ.14	storm drain:	排水管
p.16 ℓ.14	rain storm:	暴風雨
p.17 ℓ.16	gyre:	渦（巻き），回転（運動）
p.17 ℓ.16	whirlpool:	渦（巻き），混乱，騒ぎ
p.17 ℓ.16	trap:	〜をわなにかける（はめる）
p.17 ℓ.18	unlike:	〜とは違って
p.17 ℓ.18	bio-degrade:	（微生物を用いて）生物分解する
p.17 ℓ.19	break down:	正常に動かなくなる，機能停止する
p.17 ℓ.20	way to:	〜する方法，〜への方向，〜に行く道
p.17 ℓ.20	amount:	量，額，総計，総量，総額
p.17 ℓ.21	major:	主要な，重要な，大きい，多い
p.17 ℓ.21	recommendation:	推薦すること，提案，長所
p.17 ℓ.23	currently:	現在は，現在のところ，今，今や
p.17 ℓ.25	as much as:	〜するだけの量のもの，〜と同じ程度に，〜と同じ量のもの
p.17 ℓ.26	available technology:	利用可能な技術
p.17 ℓ.27	package:	（物を）荷物にまとめる，小包に作る
p.17 ℓ.28	be likely to 〜 :	〜しそうである
p.17 ℓ.28	author:	作者，著者，執筆者，作家
p.17 ℓ.29	given:	〜を考慮すると
p.17 ℓ.29	likelihood:	ありそうな状態，可能性，見込み
p.17 ℓ.29	desirability:	望ましさ，望ましい状況
p.17 ℓ.30	across-the-board:	全体（全般・全て）に渡って，全体的に，全面的に

p.17 ℓ.30　**drastic reduction**: 大幅（抜本的）な縮小（削減）
p.17 ℓ.30　**plastic packaging**: プラスチック包装
p.17 ℓ.32　**note**: 〜に注意する，気に留める，言及する，指摘する
p.17 ℓ.32　**where possible**: 可能なところで
p.17 ℓ.34　**for decades**: 数十年間
p.17 ℓ.34　**Natural Resources Defense Council**: 天然資源保護協議会（NRDC）
p.17 ℓ.35　**die from**: （人・動物が災害・けが・過労など）が原因（もと）で死ぬ（死亡する）
p.17 ℓ.35　**choke**: 息が詰まる，窒息する
p.17 ℓ.36　**intestinal blockage**: 腸閉塞
p.17 ℓ.37　**starvation**: 飢餓，餓死，飢え，窮乏

Reading Comprehension Questions

次の各文が，本文の内容に合っていればTを，合っていない場合はFを，括弧内に記入してください．

1. (　　) We have to hold a meeting about recycling by 2050.
2. (　　) The report shows that the relationship between plastics and fish will have a tendency to participate in the present circumstances.
3. (　　) More than 8 million tons of plastics every year has a measurable influence on seas of the world.
4. (　　) According to Marine Defenders, both plastic containers and other trash on the street are always carried by garbage trucks.
5. (　　) The plastic is non-biodegradable.
6. (　　) It is vitally important that we recycle plastics.
7. (　　) The report's authors recognize that the current recycling rate is all that is needed.
8. (　　) The authors provide us with the warning that we should reduce the use of plastics.
9. (　　) The Natural Resources Defense Council found out that fish eat plastics by preference.
10. (　　) Some scientists insisted that fish be dying of clashing with plastics containers.

Listening Comprehension Questions

次の英語を聴いて空欄を埋めてください．

http://learningenglish.voanews.com/a/move-to-ban-smoking-at-us-colleges-and-public-housing/3664658.html

(00:00-00:41)

New efforts are underway to make American college campuses and public housing off limits to (　　) (　　). Twenty colleges in the United States recently (　　) (　　) to help make their campuses tobacco free. And in November, U.S. Housing and Urban Development Secretary Julian Castro announced that smoking will (　　) (　　) at all public housing over the next 18 months. (　　) (　　) (　　) (　　) has over one million homes.

English Composition

次の日本文を英文に直してください．

1. 大気汚染は，多くの国で深刻な問題です．（air pollution を使って）

　

2. エネルギーを節約するため，私たちはできることをしなければならない．（save を使って）

　

3. いったんたばこを吸う癖がつくと，なかなかやめられない．（quit を使って）

ひとくちコラム

　アメリカは州による自治の裁量が大きく，独立した国に近いものがあると言われている．そのため環境対策においても各州によって温度差がある．昨今，世界的に化石燃料から脱却する機運が高まる中，アメリカ政府はシェールガスやシェールオイルを新たな産業として位置づけてきた．しかしながら，シェールガス開発においても問題点があり，開発によって引き起こされるリスクとして，「水質汚染」，「大気汚染」，「地震誘発」の3点が挙げられる．そのため，シェールガス開発に対する規制が強化されており，シェールガス開発が盛んな州の1つであるテキサス州のように，開発の内容を州規制当局に報告し，州政府のウェブサイトで公開を義務づける州もある．

Unit 5 US Political History

George Washington: President, Man, Myth

http://learningenglish.voanews.com/a/george-washington-profile/2926816.html

出典：Library Congress, Public Domain
https://cdn.loc.gov/service/pnp/cph/3a10000/3a10000/3a10200/3a10229_150px.jpg/

00:00-04:47

1 Americans call George Washington "the father of our country."
   Most people know him best as the first president of the United States, from 1789 to 1797. But the list of his accomplishments is long. Washington commanded the Continental Army in the Revolutionary War. He led the American
5 colonists to freedom from British rule. He was also president of the convention that created the U.S. Constitution.
   In his private life, Washington owned a large whiskey distillery and thousands of acres of land. He operated a large and successful farm. When the Revolutionary War was over, General Washington wanted to go home to his Virginia estate,
10 called Mount Vernon.
   Joseph Ellis is a historian and prize-winning author who wrote a book called "His Excellency: George Washington."
   "He didn't want to be president. No president in American history did not want to be president more than George Washington."

15   But other leaders asked him to become the first president under the Constitution. Every elector voted for him. Washington accepted the job as his duty.

Washington as president

When George Washington was sworn in as president in 1789, the idea of a truly united states was still just an idea. Americans were unconnected social, 20 economic and ethnic groups. For example, a quarter of the people in the state of Pennsylvania spoke only German. The new president would have to establish a social and political union under the Constitution.

But the Constitution did not say in detail how the president could do that. Doug Bradburn, founding director of the Washington Library at Mount Vernon, 25 says George Washington invented the job of president.

"I think that what people don't estimate in their scale of judging his skill as a political figure is just how fragile the country was, that the chances it would even survive were probably very, very slim."

Mr. Bradburn says President Washington set many important precedents for all 30 the presidents who followed him. First, he was not just a figurehead but a decision maker.

He established a group of advisors, the cabinet. They became a very important part of the presidency, or executive branch. Washington chose strong people to lead the departments. Sometimes those cabinet members disagreed strongly, but 35 Washington managed them well.

President Washington also established the nation's official currency and the Department of Foreign Affairs, now called the State Department. He created a six-member Supreme Court.

And, Washington said the president should set foreign policy. That responsibility 40 was not clear in the Constitution.

Mr. Bradburn says Washington took his job very seriously and always used the Constitution as his guide.

"He wasn't just trying to establish an office and then figure out a way to justify it, he was trying to work with his Constitution."

45   As president, George Washington travelled around the country. In Rhode Island, he wrote to the Hebrew Congregation at Truro. The letter spoke eloquently about the rights of Jews. Mr. Bradburn says this letter is "tremendously significant." Supporting the Jews and their religion was a revolutionary act of acceptance for its time.

読解のための語彙，文法および構文

p.21 ℓ.3	accomplishment:	功績，業績
p.21 ℓ.4	command:	指揮する
p.21 ℓ.4	the Continental Army:	大陸軍（アメリカ植民地独立のために構成された軍隊）
p.21 ℓ.4	the Revolutionary War:	独立戦争
p.21 ℓ.5	colonist:	植民地住民
p.21 ℓ.5	rule:	支配，統治
p.21 ℓ.5	convention:	集会，議会
p.21 ℓ.6	U.S. Constitution:	アメリカ合衆国憲法
p.21 ℓ.7	distillery:	蒸留所
p.21 ℓ.8	acre:	エーカー（1 acre は約 4,047 m^2）
p.21 ℓ.9	estate:	屋敷，私有地
p.21 ℓ.11	historian:	歴史家
p.21 ℓ.11	prize-winning:	受賞した
p.21 ℓ.12	His Excellency:	閣下
p.22 ℓ.16	elector:	選挙人
p.22 ℓ.18	swore:	swear（誓う）の過去形
p.22 ℓ.24	founding director:	創設者
p.22 ℓ.27	fragile:	壊れやすい，もろい
p.22 ℓ.29	precedent:	前例，慣例，先例
p.22 ℓ.30	figurehead:	名目上の長，お飾り
p.22 ℓ.30	decision maker:	決定権者
p.22 ℓ.32	cabinet:	内閣
p.22 ℓ.33	presidency:	大統領の地位，任期，職務
p.22 ℓ.33	executive:	行政上の
p.22 ℓ.33	branch:	部門
p.22 ℓ.34	department:	省
p.22 ℓ.36	currency:	通貨
p.22 ℓ.37	State Department:	国務省
p.22 ℓ.38	Supreme Court:	最高裁判所
p.22 ℓ.39	foreign policy:	外交政策
p.22 ℓ.43	justify:	正当化する
p.22 ℓ.46	eloquently:	雄弁に
p.22 ℓ.47	Jew:	ユダヤ人
p.22 ℓ.47	tremendously:	とても，非常に

Reading Comprehension Questions

次の各文が，本文の内容に合っていればTを，会っていない場合はFを，括弧内に記入してください．

1. (   ) Washington led the Continental Army in the Revolutionary War.
2. (   ) Washington was not involved with the creation of the Constitution.
3. (   ) Washington liked drinking whiskey.
4. (   ) After the Revolutionary War, Washington earned a large estate in Virginia as a reward.
5. (   ) Washington had a strong ambition to become the first president of the United States.
6. (   ) The Constitution was unclear about the responsibilities of president.
7. (   ) Washington strove a lot in order to establish the administrative system including the executive branch.
8. (   ) Foreign policy was not included in the president's responsibility in the period of Washington's administration.
9. (   ) At some times, Washington used his power beyond what the Constitution described.
10. (   ) Washington had some prejudice toward Jews.

Listening Comprehension Questions

次の英語を聴いて空欄を埋めてください．

http://learningenglish.voanews.com/a/george-washington-profile/2926816.html

(10:48-11:18)

Doug Bradburn says Washington was the right man to be the father of the country and first president. Mr. Bradburn, (   ) many historians, calls George Washington the " (   ) (   )." He made ideas about American freedom and government real, and he showed that even the president would operate (   ) (   ) (   ) of law.

English Composition

次の日本文を英文に直してください．

1. 新しい大統領は憲法下で社会的，政治的な連合体を作らなければいけないことになった．（establish を使って）

   _____

2. ワシントンは自分の仕事をとても真摯に捉えていて，指針として憲法をいつも使っていた（take を使って）

   _____

3. ワシントンは大統領が外交政策を策定するべきだと言った（set を使って）

   _____

ひとくちコラム

イギリスとの戦争に勝利した時点のアメリカは，13の州の集まりにしか過ぎず，統一的な国家とはほど遠いものだった．連邦会議という意思決定組織はあったが，財源確保のための権限が弱かったために各州の利害が優先される有様だった．大統領になる前のワシントンは，政治体制を話し合うためのフィラデルフィア会議（1787年）で議長として，統一国家の設立に尽力した．ここで，二院制，三権分立，連邦政府の権限などの仕組みが整えられた．大統領に選出されたワシントンは，5人の閣僚を任命し，連邦政府の国家機能を具体化していった．

Unit 6　　　　　　　　　　　　　　　　　　　　　　Sports

Chicago Cubs Win World Series

http://learningenglish.voanews.com/a/cubs-win-world-series/3579752.html

Chicago Cubs Win World Series
出典：Public domain Pixabay under Creative Commons CC0
https://pixabay.com/ja/%E3%82%B7%E3%82%AB%E3%82%B4-%E3%82%AB%E3%83%96%E3%82%B9-%E9%87%8E%E7%90%83-843478/

00:00-04:28

1　　This is What's Trending Today.

　　The Chicago Cubs have won baseball's World Series. It was the Cubs' first World Series win since 1908.

　　On Thursday, the hashtag #CubsWin trended across the United States.

5　　For more than 100 years, the Cubs have been known as "lovable losers." The team has many fans all across the country. But, it never seems to be able to win big games.

　　That all changed early Thursday morning in Cleveland, Ohio.

　　The Cubs defeated the Cleveland Indians 8-7 just after midnight to win the
10 World Series. The Cubs came from behind to win the series. They were losing to the Indians 3 games to 1. Then, they won three games in a row to win the World Series.

　　The series is "best-of-seven." The team that wins four out of seven games wins.

　　The results left many Cleveland fans disappointed. The Indians last won a World Series in 1948.

15　　The Cubs were one of baseball's best teams this year. But, many fans did not think they could win the series after falling behind.

One expert said the team had just a 15 percent chance of winning the series earlier in the week.

The year 2016 is turning out to be a year of unexpected winners in sports. When the Leicester City soccer team won England's championship earlier this year, some people explained its significance to American fans by comparing it to the Cubs winning the World Series. In other words, it was not expected to happen at all.

Now, a few months later, the Cubs have won.

People all over America are celebrating the victory on social media.

One of the top posts on Twitter is a photo of the sign-in sheet at a Chicago-area elementary school.

It shows that many parents told the school their child was late because they stayed up to watch the Cubs win.

Many people also liked a video showing the message board outside of Wrigley Field. That is where the Cubs play their home games in Chicago.

When the game ended, the board changed to "CUBS WIN!" and thousands of people celebrated.

Another popular Twitter post included a photo from 1993, and a prediction. It was a man's high school yearbook photo. In the text under the photo, he wrote "Chicago Cubs. 2016 World Champions. You heard it here first."

Many people cannot believe the man, who is now over 40 years old, got the prediction right.

One man in Chicago celebrated by drinking a very old beer. He had put the drink in his refrigerator in 1984. He promised not to drink it until the Cubs won a championship.

Finally, 32 years later, he was able to open the beer and drink it.

And that's What's Trending Today.

I'm Dan Friedell.

読解のための語彙，文法および構文

p.26 ℓ.2 **Chicago Cubs**: イリノイ州シカゴを本拠地とし，メジャー・リーグ・ベースボール（MLB）に加盟するチーム

p.26 ℓ.2 **baseball's World Series**: メジャー・リーグの優勝決定戦．

p.26 ℓ.4	hashtag:	＃記号と，半角英数字で構成される文字列のこと．SNS 上で使われる．
p.26 ℓ.4	trend:	ツイッターの「トレンド」になる，流行する．
p.26 ℓ.5	known as:	～として知られる
p.26 ℓ.5	lovable losers:	愛すべき敗者．カブスはファンは多いが勝てないと揶揄されてきた
p.26 ℓ.6	all across the country:	全国に
p.26 ℓ.6	seems to be:	見なされる
p.26 ℓ.8	early Thursday morning:	木曜日の未明
p.26 ℓ.9	defeat:	破る，負かす
p.26 ℓ.9	Cleveland Indians:	オハイオ州クリーブランドを本拠地とするメジャー・リーグ・ベースボールに加盟するチーム
p.26 ℓ.9	just after midnight:	深夜過ぎ
p.26 ℓ.11	in a row:	連続して
p.26 ℓ.12	best-of-seven:	7 番勝負の
p.26 ℓ.12	four out of seven:	7 試合のうち 4 試合
p.26 ℓ.13	disappointed:	落胆した
p.27 ℓ.16	fall behind:	～より遅れる，～に追い越される
p.27 ℓ.17	expert:	専門家
p.27 ℓ.18	earlier in the week:	週初め
p.27 ℓ.19	turn out to be:	～という結果となる
p.27 ℓ.19	unexpected winner:	予想外の勝者
p.27 ℓ.20	Leicester City soccer team:	イングランド 1 部プレミア・リーグに所属するサッカーチーム，2015/2016 年シーズンで奇跡の優勝を果たした．
p.27 ℓ.20	earlier this year:	今年の初め
p.27 ℓ.21	significance:	重要性
p.27 ℓ.22	in other words:	言い換えると
p.27 ℓ.25	post:	ツイッターやフェイスブックでの投稿
p.27 ℓ.25	sign-in sheet:	学校に立ち入る際に名前や目的を記入する用紙
p.27 ℓ.28	stay up:	夜遅くまで起きている
p.27 ℓ.29	message board:	メッセージボード，伝言板
p.27 ℓ.29	Wrigley Field:	シカゴ・カブスの本拠地球場
p.27 ℓ.34	prediction:	予言
p.27 ℓ.35	year book:	卒業アルバム
p.27 ℓ.40	refrigerator:	冷蔵庫
p.27 ℓ.42	finally:	ついに，とうとう，最終的に

Reading Comprehension Questions

次の各文が，本文の内容に合っていればＴを，会っていない場合はＦを，括弧内に記入してください．

1. (　　) The Chicago Cubs won the World Series for the first time since 1908.
2. (　　) Although the Cubs are not necessarily a competitive team, they have a lot of fans across the country.
3. (　　) To win a World Series, the team has to win seven games.
4. (　　) The Cleveland Indians won only one game in the World Series.
5. (　　) The Cleveland Indians has not won a World Series for more than half a century.
6. (　　) The Chicago Cubs also defeated the Leicester City in the England's championship in 2016.
7. (　　) At an elementary school in Chicago, parents told that their children stayed up late to support the Cubs on TV.
8. (　　) Wrigley Field is a soccer stadium and it held a public viewing for the Cubs fans.
9. (　　) One Cubs fan wrote in his high school year book in 1993 that the Cubs would win the World Series.
10. (　　) Another Cubs fan had kept a beer in the refrigerator since 1984, promising that he would not drink it until the Cubs won a World Series.

Listening Comprehension Questions

次の英語を聴いて空欄を埋めてください

http://learningenglish.voanews.com/a/cubs-win-world-series/3579752.html

[01:58-02:28]

The year 2016 (　　　　) (　　　　　) (　　　　　　) to be a year of unexpected winners in sports. When the Leicester City soccer team won England's championship earlier this year, some people explained (　　　　　) (　　　　　) to American fans by (　　　　) (　　　　　) (　　　　　) the Cubs winning the World Series. In other words, it was not expected to happen at all.

English Composition

次の日本文を英文に直してください．

1. シカゴ・カブスは3連勝を果たし，ワールドシリーズを制覇した．（in a row を使って）

2. 2016年はスポーツで予想外のチームが優勝をしたことが重なる年になりつつある．（turn out を使って）

3. 彼はカブスが優勝するまでそれ（beer）を飲まないと約束したのだった．（promise を使って）

ひとくちコラム

　アメリカで人気のスポーツと言えば，フットボール，ホッケー，バスケットボール，そしてベースボールだ．1903年にメジャー・リーグが発足し，1920年代にはラジオで実況されるようになり，国民的スポーツになった．初期のスーパースターにはホームラン・バッターのベイブ・ルースがいる．

　今日のMLBは人種も国籍も多様化しているが，第二次世界大戦までは黒人がプレーすることはできなかった．だから，MLBとは別に黒人リーグが存在した．この人種障壁を乗り越えた最初の黒人MLB選手がジャッキー・ロビンソンで，1947年にブルックリン・ドジャースの一塁手としてメジャー・デビューした．

　ベースボールから生まれたイディオムに，ballpark figure がある．昔，各球団は入場者数をおおまかに数えていたことから，「だいたいの数字」という意味で，ビジネスなどでも使われる．

Unit 7

Public Welfare

Program Helps Lift American Families Out of Poverty

http://learningenglish.voanews.com/a/program-helps-lift-american-families-out-of-poverty/3570024.html

Program Helps Lift American Families Out of Poverty
出典：VOA, Public Domain
http://av.voanews.com/Videoroot/Pangeavideo/2016/10/
e/ec/ec5c7125-850c-42de-a58b-d21de982beab.mp4

00:00-04:08

1   A program designed to help families escape poverty in the American state of Georgia is serving as a model for other parts of the United States.

The program is a partnership between private donors and the city government in Atlanta, Georgia's capital.

5   Today, the East Lake neighborhood of Atlanta is a nice place to live. But 20 years ago the neighborhood was unsafe and looked unappealing.

Recently, VOA reporter Chris Simkins visited East Lake and spoke with Daniel Shoy, the president of the East Lake Foundation. The foundation was set up to help people in the community.

10   "More than 20 years ago this was the home to East Lake Meadows, which was one of the nation's most violent housing developments, and today is probably one of the most promising."

The city and private charities are spending $150 million to help poor families escape poverty.

15   Carol Naughton works for a non-profit group called Purpose Built Communities. It works with local leaders to help improve communities.

"The absolute idea of income inequality is part of the problem, but the lack of social mobility is just as big a problem. If people in America don't feel like they have a reasonable shot at working and earning a better life and creating a better opportunity for their children, I think our democracy is threatened at its very core."

East Lake Village is home to about 2,100 people. Only low or middle-income individuals are permitted to live there. The housing development has banks, a grocery store and other businesses usually found in higher income neighborhoods.

Young people in East Lake are given help with their education so they can go to college and get a good job.

Twenty years ago, an average family of four in this neighborhood struggled to earn $4,500 a year. Shoy says the average income is now about $20,000.

"There was only 14 percent employment in this community. Now we see a hundred percent employment for the families that we work with who are living in the subsidized units. We've seen a dramatic increase in annual household income."

Michelle Campbell and her family have experienced success since they moved to East Lake in 2013. Campbell helps operate the housing development. She is building wealth and will soon buy her first home.

"This type of program encourage self-sufficiency. It is a move-to-work program, so the residents are required to work 30 hours or more in order to be on the program. And the goal is geared to them getting off the program, finding a home, getting into a better position financially."

East Lake leaders say its success can be a model for what is possible when people come together to end poverty.

読解のための語彙，文法および構文

p.31 ℓ.1	program:	行政計画
p.31 ℓ.1	escape poverty:	貧困から脱出する
p.31 ℓ.2	model:	見本
p.31 ℓ.3	private:	個人の
p.31 ℓ.4	capital:	州都．首都という意味もある．
p.31 ℓ.5	neighborhood:	近所，近隣地，地方
p.31 ℓ.6	unappealing:	魅力がない，目立たない

Unit 7 Program Helps Lift American Families Out of Poverty *33*

p.31 ℓ.7　speak with: 〜と話す ここでは, Chris Simkinsがリポーターという立場なので, 「取材する」の意味.

p.31 ℓ.11　housing development: 集団住宅

p.31 ℓ.11　probably: おそらく

p.31 ℓ.12　promising: 将来について希望が持てる（形容詞）

p.32 ℓ.18　mobility: 流動性, 可動性. 社会学の用語で, 人生の中で社会的階級を移動することを指す.

p.32 ℓ.19　reasonable shot: reasonableは道理にあった, 正当な, という意味を持ち, shotは一般に銃でうつことを指すが, ここではshotを目標とした.

p.32 ℓ.31　subsidized: subsidize 〜に助成金を支援する

p.32 ℓ.31　unit: 家, 一戸

p.32 ℓ.36　self-sufficiency: 自給自足. ここでは経済的に自立するという意味.

p.32 ℓ.37　residents: 住居者

p.32 ℓ.37　be on: 参加する

p.32 ℓ.38　get off: 離れる

p.32 ℓ.39　financially: 金銭的に

Reading Comprehension Questions

次の各文が, 本文の内容に合っていればTを, 会っていない場合はFを, 括弧内に記入してください.

1. (　) The program is designed to help families with economic problems.
2. (　) The program is funded by private donations and the city government.
3. (　) East Lake in Georgia has long been an attractive place to live.
4. (　) The East Lake Foundation helps people set up their community-based businesses.
5. (　) In the past 20 years, there has been a huge improvement in East Lake.
6. (　) Purpose Built Communities is a non-profit organization to educate local leaders.
7. (　) Carol Naughton says that the problem is not just income inequality, but also the lack of social mobility.
8. (　) In this community, the average income of four-person family has risen to $20,000 from $4,500 in the past 20 years.
9. (　) One of the successful families in the community is Michelle Campbell's, who moved to East Lake in 2013.

10. (　　) Michelle Campbell says that the program in East Lake requires at least 30-hour work to get a home.

Listening Comprehension Questions

次の英語を聴いて空欄を埋めてください．

http://learningenglish.voanews.com/a/program-helps-lift-american-families-out-of-poverty/3570024.html

[01:39-01:58]

The absolute idea of (　　　　) (　　　　) is part of the problem, but the lack of (　　　　) (　　　　) is just as big a problem. If people in America don't feel like they have a reasonable **shot** at working and (　　　　) (　　　　) (　　　　) (　　　　) and creating a better opportunity for their children, I think our democracy (　　　　) (　　　　) at its very **core**.

English Composition

次の日本文を英文に直してください．

1. 貧困から逃れたい家庭を助けるためのプログラムがアメリカのジョージア州で行われており，他州の見本となっている．（help を使って）

2. 20年前は，この地域の平均的な4人家族は4,500ドルを稼ぐのに苦労していた．（struggle を使って）

3. 住居者はプログラムの対象でいるためには、（週）30時間の労働を義務づけられます．（require を使って）

ひとくちコラム

　貧困層に対する行政主導の住宅補助のことを public housing あるいは housing project と呼ぶ．市や州が低所得者向けの集合住宅を建設し，相場より安い家賃でアパートを提供することで，彼らを経済的に援助する行政サービスのことである．その起源は19世紀終わりまで遡ることができ，1930年代の大恐慌期には連邦政府が積極的に関与した．社会的関心がもたれるようになるのは1960年代以降である．なぜなら，さまざまな弊害が発生したからである．たとえば，特定地区に貧困層が集中して住むことになるため，治安が悪化しスラム化する例が全国で発生した．20年前のイースト・レイク地区はその典型だった．しかし，今日では自助努力を組み入れることにより，居住者の経済的自立を手助けし，良好な住環境を実現している．

Unit 8

Agriculture

Robot Can Help With Farm Work

http://learningenglish.voanews.com/a/robots-can-help-with-farm-work/3576587.html

Robot Can Help With Farm Work
出典：VOA, Public Domain
http://learningenglish.voanews.com/a/robots-can-help-with-farm-work/3576587.html

00:00-04:02

1   In the American state of Idaho, a robot moves between lines of fruit trees and grapevines. It is doing farm work.

　Called "IdaBot," this robot is a prototype, or model. An engineering team at Northwest Nazarene University in Nampa, Idaho, developed IdaBot.

5   It looks like a small military tank. But, it is armed with cameras and radio frequency sensors instead of guns. It moves slowly through an orchard, spraying chemicals on each plant that needs treatment.

　It can do other jobs too, including watching over crops and harvesting them.

How the robot works

10   The robot uses radio frequency identification in its work. This process uses electronic devices on the trees or grapevines to identify them. As the IdaBot moves through the orchards, it "reads" the devices on the plants to learn what it needs.

　Josh Griffin is one of the project leaders. He explains how the robot works.

　"You can program into the IdaBot, trees number one, and trees number five
15 need chemicals. Each tree will have a radio frequency identification tag on it. The IdaBot would use the signal from the tag to determine which tree it is next to. When

it is next to tree five, it will spray chemicals on tree number five, when it is on tree number one, it will spray the chemicals there."

Griffin, an assistant engineering professor, says the robot can work on its own. It can also work with other technology, like drones – small pilotless planes.

In an experiment, a drone carried a special camera that captures images of grapevines or fruit trees. The image information is processed through a computer program. The color of the image lets the robot know how much chemical the plants need.

Griffin says the robot can help farmers save money on labor. It also saves money by reducing the use of chemicals. And that helps the environment.

"It automatically, without human intervention, applies the chemicals and then it does so in very low pressure. So, it does so very precisely. The chemicals go where you want them to go, not over spraying to other areas."

Fruit Counting Application

The robot team of students and professors is also developing a Fruit Counting Application for the IdaBot. It uses a vision system to correctly estimate the size of the fruit crop.

Duke Bulanon, another assistant engineering professor, works with Griffin on the project. He explains that the system will use several different kinds of cameras- color, near-infrared and stereo cameras. They will take images from each tree as IdaBot moves along the orchard.

"Then we will use those images and create a computer program to estimate the number of fruits on each tree."

Farmer Michael Williamson owns an orchard in Caldwell, Idaho. He says he is looking forward to trying out the computer program on his trees.

読解のための語彙，文法および構文

- p.36 ℓ.1　state: 州
- p.36 ℓ.2　grapevine: ぶどうの木
- p.36 ℓ.2　farm work: 農作業
- p.36 ℓ.3　prototype:（〜の）原型，典型，試作品
- p.36 ℓ.4　Northwest Nazarene University in Nampa, Idaho: アイダホ州のナンパにあるノースウェスト・ナザリーン大学
- p.36 ℓ.5　look like: 〜のように見える，〜に似ている

p.36 ℓ.5	military tank:	戦車
p.36 ℓ.5	armed with:	搭載する
p.36 ℓ.5	radio frequency sensors:	無線周波数センサー
p.36 ℓ.6	through:	～を通じて，～の至るところを
p.36 ℓ.6	orchard:	果樹園
p.36 ℓ.6	instead of:	～の代わりに
p.36 ℓ.7	chemicals:	化学薬品
p.36 ℓ.8	watch over:	～を世話する，守る，担当する
p.36 ℓ.9	harvesting:	収穫．
p.36 ℓ.10	radio frequency identification:	無線周波数識別装置
p.36 ℓ.11	electronic devices:	電子機器
p.36 ℓ.11	to identify them:	それらを識別するために
p.36 ℓ.11	As the IdaBot moves through the orchards:	アイダボットは果樹園の至るところを移動している時
p.36 ℓ.12	to learn what it needs:	それが何を必要としているかを学ぶために
p.36 ℓ.14	You can program into the IdaBot:	あなたはアイダボットの中にプログラムをすることができる．
p.36 ℓ.14	trees number one:	（木の一本一本に識別番号が付けられていて）1番の木
p.36 ℓ.15	each:	それぞれ，おのおの
p.36 ℓ.16	next to:	～の隣に
p.37 ℓ.19	assistant professor:	助教授
p.37 ℓ.19	on its own:	単独で
p.37 ℓ.21	experiment:	実験
p.37 ℓ.22	be processed:	～を（コンピューター）で処理する
p.37 ℓ.25	money on labor:	人件費
p.37 ℓ.26	reducing the use of chemicals:	化学薬品の使用を減らす
p.37 ℓ.27	automatically:	自動的に
p.37 ℓ.27	human intervention:	人間の干渉
p.37 ℓ.28	precisely:	正確に，はっきりと
p.37 ℓ.32	correctly estimate:	正確に見積もる
p.37 ℓ.35	several different kinds of camera:	複数の違う種類のカメラ
p.37 ℓ.36	near-infrared:	近赤外線
p.37 ℓ.36	as IdaBot moves along the orchard:	アイダボットが果樹園の中を移動している時に

Reading Comprehension Questions

次の各文が，本文の内容に合っていればTを，会っていない場合はFを，括弧内に記入してください．

1. (　　) A university in Idaho created a robot called IdaBot.
2. (　　) The IdaBot has arms loaded with cameras, radio frequency sensors, and guns.
3. (　　) The robot can move between fruit trees to spray chemicals.
4. (　　) The robot also harvests crops.
5. (　　) Using radio frequency identification, the robot can identify each tree.
6. (　　) Josh Griffin is a farmer and leading the IdaBot project.
7. (　　) The robot can be used with other robots such as drones.
8. (　　) One of the benefits of IdaBot is that it is eco-friendly, for example, reducing the amount of chemicals.
9. (　　) Now the robot team is trying to sell the IdaBot to other states.
10. (　　) Fruit Counting Application will analyze images of each tree to calculate how many fruits each tree has.

Listening Comprehension Questions

次の英語を聴いて空欄を埋めてください．

http://learningenglish.voanews.com/a/robots-can-help-with-farm-work/3576587.html

04:48-05:10

(本文のあとにつづく部分)
(　　　　　) (　　　　　) (　　　　　) (　　　　　) have to pay for this robot? Big pieces of farm equipment can be expensive. But Griffin estimates a basic IdaBot that uses (　　　　　) (　　　　　) (　　　　　) (　　　　　) would be relatively low-cost.

English Composition

次の日本文を英文に直してください．

1. それは小さい戦車のように見える（looks like を使って）

2. この処理には樹木やぶどうの蔓に取り付けられた電子機器を使って識別する．（identify を使って）

　　_____

3. 5 番の隣にあるときは，アイダボットは 5 番の樹に化学薬品を吹きかけます．（next to を使って）

　　_____

ひとくちコラム

　経済先進国の例にもれず，アメリカでも国全体の労働人口にしめる農業従事者の割合は少なくなってきている．しかし，アメリカ農業は産業として強さを維持している．国全体として広大な農地を有するだけでなく，経営合理化・ハイテク化を追求しているからである．まず，一農家あたりの農地面積が増加することにより，機械化導入が可能になり経営合理化を行っている．さらにテクノロジーが種まき，殺虫，散水，収穫などの各段階で導入される．例えば，飛行機で種を蒔き，殺虫剤を空中散布し，ロボットを使って収穫するという具合である．近年では，遺伝子操作を含むバイオテクノロジーが注目を浴びている．安全性，倫理面からバイオテクノロジーに対して慎重な意見も聞かれる．

Unit 9 Politics

2016 US Election is Hard for Civics Teachers

http://learningenglish.voanews.com/a/us-election-is-hard-for-civics-teachers/3576557.html

2016 US Election is Hard for Civics Teachers
出典：VOA, Public Domain
http://learningenglish.voanews.com/a/us-election-is-hard-for-civics-teachers/3576557.html

(00:00-03:19)

1   Has the American election campaign been difficult to watch?
    Imagine if you had to explain it to a class of middle school students.
    Every four years, teachers in the United States explain how the government works by talking with students about the presidential campaign.
5   But this year, some civics teachers report having difficulty when discussing the campaign. They had to explain concerns about candidates' behavior and a lack of substance in the political debate.
    Javaughn Perkins is a teacher at George Washington Middle School in Alexandria, Virginia. He likes to have students watch campaign advertisements to
10 look for their tools of persuasion.
    Perkins thinks that by the age of 12 or 13 years, students are at a good age to start learning about government. However, the ups and downs of the election campaign has made this year more difficult.
    "There used to be a time when I could literally come in, we'd pop on the
15 Washington Post (newspaper) or CNN or any of the other websites, and I could just go right to the front page and [say], 'Let's have a conversation.'"

Perkins says that this year, newspaper stories are not always a good subject for 8th grade students. One example is the leaked video of candidate Donald Trump talking about sexually harassing women.

When Trump made fun of a disabled person, Perkins was again not sure how to talk about it with his class.

"When that initially broke, I had some thoughts about coming in and us having a conversation, and I held off."

Perkins felt that it would have directed students' attention away from teaching government, and would not have helped the school's anti-bullying efforts.

Students noticing the difference

Students appear to be noticing the problem, too. When Perkins asked his students how the campaigns have changed over the years, they felt that the political climate has changed. They said it now is more harmful --or bad -- than before.

"The older candidates were more formal, more structured. They mainly focused on topics that were concerning at the time such as wars. But now they're just like, 'Let's point as many fingers as we can at the other person.' It's childish! It's ridiculous! It's an embarrassment to this country!"

Perkins says the lack of discussion on major issues in the campaign has made his job harder.

"I've had less and less to choose from that will actually, again, get at the issues, even the candidates, in a very real way."

| 読解のための語彙，文法および構文 |

- *p.41 ℓ.1* election campaign: 選挙戦
- *p.41 ℓ.2* middle school: 中学校．アメリカの初等・中等教育課程では，primary school, middle school, high school とよぶのが一般的．
- *p.41 ℓ.4* presidential campaign: 大統領選挙
- *p.41 ℓ.5* civics: 公民科，倫理社会
- *p.41 ℓ.5* have difficulty: 問題を抱えている，苦労する
- *p.41 ℓ.10* persuasion: 説得
- *p.41 ℓ.12* the ups and downs: 良いこと悪いことが合い重なる状態．
- *p.41 ℓ.14* literally: 文字通りに，（強意語として）本当に，まったく
- *p.41 ℓ.14* come in: （話題を）持ち出す

p.41 ℓ.14	pop on:	電気機器などをオンにする.
p.42 ℓ.18	8th grade:	8年生. アメリカでは，学年を小学1年からの通算でかぞえる．日本で言えば，中学2年生.
p.42 ℓ.19	harass:	困らす，悩ます
p.42 ℓ.20	made fun of:	からかう.
p.42 ℓ.20	disabled person:	障がい者. 他にも，challenged person という言い方もある.
p.42 ℓ.23	held off:	ためらう
p.42 ℓ.24	direct students' attention away from teaching government:	政府について教えることから生徒の関心をそらさせる
p.42 ℓ.25	bullying:	いじめ
p.42 ℓ.29	political climate:	政治状況
p.42 ℓ.31	formal:	（人間として）礼節を保っている
p.42 ℓ.31	structured:	（議論などにおいて）筋が通っている
p.42 ℓ.33	point as many fingers:	非難する．finger-pointing という言い方があり，他人を批判することを意味する.
p.42 ℓ.35	major issues:	重要議題
p.42 ℓ.37	get at:	知る，確かめる

Reading Comprehension Questions

次の各文が，本文の内容に合っていればTを，会っていない場合はFを，括弧内に記入してください．

1. (　　) Every four years, American schools hold a campaign to decide which candidate they support for the next president of the United States.
2. (　　) Javaughn Perkins teaches at a middle school in Washington.
3. (　　) Perkins uses presidential campaign advertisements as his classroom materials to encourage his students to think about how much convincing they are.
4. (　　) The election campaign in 2016, according to Perkins, is not suitable to teach students.
5. (　　) Perkins used to use media websites for classroom discussion.
6. (　　) One of the major reasons Perkins hesitates using media coverage this year is that candidate Trump uses offensive language toward particular people.
7. (　　) Perkins's students are aware of the change of political system over

the years.

8. (　) Perkins thinks that this year's presidential campaign is too difficult for students to understand.
9. (　) The difference between older candidates and this year's is that the former was more topic-focused while the latter is more focused on attacking the other candidate.
10. (　) The growing popularity of candidate Trump makes teaching job less and less secure.

Listening Comprehension Questions

次の英語を聴いて空欄を埋めてください．

http://learningenglish.voanews.com/a/us-election-is-hard-for-civics-teachers/3576557.html

[03:21-04:00]

（本文のあとにつづく部分）

While many teachers like to have **mock** debates in the classroom (　　　　) (　　　　) (　　　　　　), even that exercise is risky. Brent Wathke, a teacher at DeLong Middle School, told *The New York Times* that (　　　　) (　　　　) (　　　　) (　　　　　) students to say insulting words. Instead, he had his class talk about the election campaign using "Socratic circles." He (　　　　) (　　　　) (　　　　) (　　　　) small groups, and had them use work sheets to answer questions that he asked.

English Composition

次の日本文を英文に直してください．

1. 4年ごとに，アメリカの教師たちは政府の役割を説明するのに，大統領選挙について生徒たちと話し合う．（presidential campaign を使って）

2. 彼らはおもに戦争などの重要課題に重点を置いていた（focus on を使って）

3. トランプが身体障がい者をからかったとき，パーキンスはどうやってこのことを授業で話せばよいのか分からなかった．（a disabled person を使って）

> **ひとくちコラム**
>
> アメリカの大統領を選ぶ仕組みは独特である．11月初旬の火曜日に各州で投票が行われるのだが，実はこのとき有権者は立候補者を選ぶのではなく，選挙人（elector）に票を投じる．選挙人とは，12月の本選挙で投票する人のことで，どの候補に投票するかを表明している．選挙人の数は州により違う（人口に比例させて人数が決まる）．面白いのは，12月の本選挙では，各州の選挙人団（Electoral College）が大統領候補に投票するとき，選挙人団全員がその州で得票数の多かった候補に票を投じる点である（例外としてネブラスカ州とメイン州）．要するに，接戦で勝とうが大差で勝とうが，得られる票数は同じことになる．この方式だと，総得票数が多い候補が負けるということが起きる．2016年の大統領選挙がまさにそうだった．

Unit 10

Culture

Hold The Butter! Modern Diets Meet Holiday Traditions

http://learningenglish.voanews.com/a/hold-the-butter-modern-diets-meet-holiday-traditions/3117341.html

出典：VOA, Public Domain
http://learningenglish.voanews.com/a/hold-the-butter-modern-diets-meet-holiday-traditions/3117341.html

00:00-03:09

1   Rich, heavy food is a major part of the end of the year holidays in the United States.

People in the US celebrate Thanksgiving on the third Thursday of November. People around the world celebrate Christmas on December 25.

5   Both holidays involve traditions of cooking large meals. The food at these meals usually has lots of sugar, salt and butter in it. Turkey and pie are some of the most common foods at these holidays.

Terri Price has hosted a holiday party on the last Saturday before every Christmas for 30 years.

10   "It started when my children were very, very small. In fact, there was only one of them. And it's sort of my Christmas gift to me. Many of the dishes I have been preparing for most of the 30 years."

But over time, some traditions do change. The Neveldines are a family who hope to be healthier by changing what they eat. Mick Fury, the Neveldine's oldest
15 child, said this change is important during the holidays and the rest of the year, too.

"The holidays are actually, sort of, the most exciting time because it's a chance to see if we can achieve traditional dishes in a way that is organic and healthy and fun. And maybe, we don't tell people. Like, 'Hey! Here's turkey dinner!' But then, it turns out, if they love it we tell them, 'It's organic. It's great.'"

20　　Mick and his girlfriend, Michelle, try to eat only organic food. Organic food is any plant or animal food product made without the use of unnatural chemicals or processes.

　　The United States Department of Agriculture, or USDA, is the part of the U.S. government that creates laws about food. The USDA began identifying which foods 25 are organic in 2002.

　　Mick chose to eat only organic food after his girlfriend found she felt sick when eating gluten. Gluten is in products which include wheat. Mick began looking more closely at the ingredients in the food he bought. The amount of unnatural ingredients in most food surprised him.

30　　But, Mick is not the only Neveldine who changed their diet. Felicia Neveldine, Mick's sister, decided nine years ago to become a vegan. A vegan is a person who does not eat or use animal products of any kind.

　　Felicia became a vegan because of her concern for the treatment of animals and the environmental effects of animal farming. She said that her change in diet also 35 improved her health.

　　"I used to have a lot of problems with my stomach and digestion and since I became a vegan, I feel just better every day."

　　Choosing these special diets means the Neveldines choose their foods carefully. Mick grows a garden behind his home where he gets fresh vegetables. They also 40 make traditional holiday food like mashed potatoes without milk or butter.

読解のための語彙，文法および構文

- *p.46 ℓ.1*　**rich, heavy food:** 贅沢で大量の食事
- *p.46 ℓ.1*　**major part:** 主要行事（この箇所は行事の中でメインとなっている部分 → 主要行事と考える）
- *p.46 ℓ.3*　**celebrate Thanksgiving:** 感謝祭を祝う
- *p.46 ℓ.5*　**involve traditions of cooking large meals:** ごちそうを作る伝統がある．
- *p.46 ℓ.6*　**Turkey:** 七面鳥
- *p.46 ℓ.11*　**sort of:** のようなもの
- *p.46 ℓ.11*　**many of the dishes:** 多くの料理

p.46 ℓ.11	I have been preparing for most of the 30 years: 30年間の大半は準備に費やしてきた
p.46 ℓ.13	over time: 時が経つにつれて
p.46 ℓ.13	traditions: 伝統
p.46 ℓ.14	oldest child: 第一子
p.46 ℓ.15	during the holidays: 休暇中
p.46 ℓ.15	the rest of the year: 一年を通じた他の日
p.46 ℓ.17	achieve traditional dishes in a way that is organic and healthy and fun: 有機栽培の健康的で楽しい方法で伝統料理を食べることができる.「achieve」は「伝統料理にありつく」→「伝統料理を食べる」の「食べる」と意訳すると意味が取りやすい.
p.47 ℓ.19	it turns out: 〜と分かる
p.47 ℓ.20	organic food: 自然食品
p.47 ℓ.21	without the use of unnatural chemicals or processes.: 不自然な化学物質の添加や加工を行わずに
p.47 ℓ.23	the United States Department of Agriculture, or USDA: 米国農務省（USDA）
p.47 ℓ.24	creates laws: 法律を制定する
p.47 ℓ.24	began identifying which foods are organic: どの食品が自然食品かの特定を開始した
p.47 ℓ.27	gluten: グルテン
p.47 ℓ.28	ingredients in the food: 食品の成分
p.47 ℓ.29	unnatural ingredients: 不自然な成分
p.47 ℓ.31	vegan: 完全菜食主義者.
p.47 ℓ.33	her concern for the treatment of animals and the environmental effects of animal farming: 動物の扱いと動物農場の環境への影響を懸念して
p.47 ℓ.36	stomach and digestion: 胃や消化力
p.47 ℓ.38	choose their foods carefully: 慎重に食べ物を選ぶ
p.47 ℓ.39	a garden behind his home: 自宅の裏にある庭
p.47 ℓ.40	mashed potatoes: マッシュポテト

Reading Comprehension Questions

次の各文が，本文の内容に合っていればTを，合っていない場合はFを，括弧内に記入してください．

1. (　　) Rich, heavy food is a major part of the end of the year holidays in the United States.

2. (　　) Both holidays don't involve traditions of cooking large meals.
3. (　　) Terri Price has hosted a holiday party on the last Saturday.
4. (　　) The Neveldines are a family who don't hope to be healthier by changing what they eat.
5. (　　) Mick and his girlfriend, Michelle, try to eat only organic food.
6. (　　) The USDA began identifying which foods are organic in 2002
7. (　　) Mick chose to eat only organic food after his girlfriend found she did not feel sick when eating gluten.
8. (　　) Mick is the only Neveldine who changed their diet.
9. (　　) Felicia did not become a vegan because of her concern for the treatment of animals.
10. (　　) Mick grows a garden behind his home.

Listening Comprehension Questions

次の英語を聴いて空欄を埋めてください．

http://learningenglish.voanews.com/pp/3117424/ppt0.html

(04:07-04:28)

Studies (　　　　) that high (　　　　) diets can (　　　　) people to (　　　　) overweight. The Centers for Disease Control, or CDC, is the top national (　　　　) (　　　　) organization in the U.S. A 2014 report from the CDC (　　　　) (　　　　) percent of adults in the U.S. over (　　　) years old are (　　　　　).

English Composition

1. 米国の人々は11月の第3木曜日に感謝祭を祝う．(celebrate を使って)

2. ミックは自分が買った食品の成分をもっと詳しく調べ始めた．(look more closel を使って)

3. フェリシアは，動物の扱いと動物農場の環境への影響を懸念して完全菜食主義者になった．(because of one's concern for を使って)

> **ひとくちコラム**
>
> 感謝祭は米国では毎年 11 月の第 4 木曜日であり祝日となる．現代の感謝祭は宗教的な意味合いは弱く，友人が集まる食事会だったり，家族が皆集まったりする行事のひとつとなっている．実際に感謝祭当日は商店街も閑散としていることが多い．この状況からも感謝祭が行楽のための祝日ではなく，家族や親戚，友人が集うためのものであることが分かる．七面鳥を食べる習慣があるが，実際にはそれに縛られず，ごちそうを食べながら，集まった友人や家族と会話を楽しむ日となっている．

Unit 11   Public Health and Social Security

One-Third of U.S. Counties Have More Deaths than Births

http://learningenglish.voanews.com/a/one-third-of-us-counties-have-more-deaths-than-births/3574388.html

出典：Public domain Pixabay under Creative Commons CC0
https://pixabay.com/ja/

00:00-04:37

1　　Recently, we reported on the importance of counties in the United States.

Today we have a lot more on what the U.S. Census Bureau calls "the primary political and administrative divisions of states."

There are more than 3,000 counties nationwide.

5　　Most states use the word "county" to describe these subdivisions, or separate areas, within a larger territory. Naturally, there are exceptions to this definition. For example, the southern state of Louisiana is divided up into parishes.

The Census Bureau reports that 1,653 counties lost population between 2010 and 2015. That is more than half of all counties nationwide. At the same time, the 10 general population grew by about 4 percent.

Delaware and Hawaii are the only two states that did not have a single county with a falling population number.

If not for new immigrants, 194 more U.S. counties would have lost population.

More people are dying than are being born in more than one-third of all counties. 15 Population experts call this "natural decrease." But that does not always mean their population is shrinking.

In 2009, the Census Bureau reported natural decrease in 880 counties. can grow even when there are more deaths than births. The reason? People are moving there from other parts of the United States or from other countries.

Some news stories have described counties that record more deaths than births as "dying counties." In 2009, the Census Bureau reported natural decrease in 880 counties. In 2012, the Census Bureau estimated natural decrease in 1,135 counties. Most were in rural areas.

Kenneth Johnson is a professor of sociology at the University of New Hampshire. He told the Associated Press that the number of counties with natural decrease is rising not only because there are fewer births than deaths in those areas. He said another reason is an increase in the number of deaths among "baby boomers." The term baby boomer is used to describe the 70 million Americans who were born between 1946 and 1964.

Johnson said, "I expect natural decrease to remain high in the future. These counties are in a pretty steep downward spiral. The young people leave and the older adults stay in place and age."

He adds, "that unless something major changes -- for instance, new development such as a meatpacking plant to attract young Hispanics -- these areas are likely to have more and more natural decrease."

About 46 percent of rural counties experienced natural decrease. That compares to 17 percent of counties in populated areas.

Experts say counties "die" because they have increasingly-older populations, a low birth rate and a poor economy. They say it is difficult for some areas to retain or attract younger people.

Japan and many European countries have been experiencing natural decrease for many years.

In the United States, the 10 largest counties are in the West, in states such as California, Arizona and Nevada. Some of the smallest counties are in eastern states.

読解のための語彙，文法および構文

p.51 ℓ.1　recently: 最近

p.51 ℓ.1　counties: 郡．米国は50州と首都ワシントンDCがあるコロンビア特別区に分かれている．州の下位行政区分として郡があり，地方自治を行っている．

p.51 ℓ.2　a lot more: さらに多くの

Unit 11 One-Third of U.S. Counties Have More Deaths than Births   53

p.51 ℓ.2   U.S. Census Bureau: 米国国勢調査局
p.51 ℓ.3   nationwide: 全国の
p.51 ℓ.5   subdivisions: 下位区分
p.51 ℓ.6   exceptions: 例外
p.51 ℓ.7   divided up into parishes: 教区に分かれている
p.51 ℓ.8   population: 人口
p.51 ℓ.9   more than half of all counties nationwide: 全国の郡全数の半分を超える
p.51 ℓ.9   At the same time: 同時に
p.51 ℓ.11 Delaware and Hawaii: デラウェア州とハワイ州
p.51 ℓ.14 in more than one-third of all counties: 全数の3分の1を越える郡で
p.51 ℓ.15 natural decrease: 自然減少
p.51 ℓ.16 population is shrinking: 人口が減少している
p.52 ℓ.19 from other parts of the United States or from other countries.
p.52 ℓ.21 dying counties: 瀕死の郡
p.52 ℓ.22 estimated: 概算した
p.52 ℓ.23 in rural areas: 農村部
p.52 ℓ.25 Associated Press: AP通信
p.52 ℓ.26 not only: だけではなく．通常「not only ～ but also」という形で使うが，この課題では「not only」で使っている．
p.52 ℓ.27 baby boomers: ベビーブーマー．説明はその用語以降で行われている．
p.52 ℓ.30 remain high: 「decrease」が将来にわたり高い比率で続いていくことを述べているいる．急降下が続くという意味．
p.52 ℓ.31 pretty steep downward spiral: 急降下するスパイラル状態
p.52 ℓ.33 unless: ～がなければ
p.52 ℓ.34 are likely to ～ : ～する可能性が高い
p.52 ℓ.38 they have increasingly-older populations: 住民がますます高齢化する
p.52 ℓ.43 in the West: 西部に

Reading Comprehension Questions

次の各文が，本文の内容に合っていればTを，合っていない場合はFを，括弧内に記入してください．

1. (   ) There are more than 3,000 counties nationwide.
2. (   ) Most states use the word "county" to describe these subdivisions, or separate areas, within a larger territory.

3. (　) The Census Bureau reports that 1,653 counties increased population between 2010 and 2015.
4. (　) Delaware and California are the only two states that did not have a single county with a falling population number.
5. (　) More people are dying than are being born in more than one-third of all counties.
6. (　) A county's population cannot grow even when there are more deaths than births.
7. (　) In 2009, the Census Bureau reported natural decrease in 880 counties.
8. (　) The term baby boomer is used to describe the 70 million Americans who were born between 1996 and 2004.
9. (　) About 66 percent of rural counties experienced natural decrease.
10. (　) Japan and many European countries have been experiencing natural decrease for many years.

Listening Comprehension Questions

次の英語を聴いて空欄を埋めてください．

http://learningenglish.voanews.com/pp/3574541/ppt0.html

[05:16-05:40]

Five of the (　　) smallest (　　　) by (　　　) (　　) in the state of Nebraska. Cook County, Illinois, which (　　　) Chicago, is the second-most-populous county in the nation. It (　　) more (　　　) than 29 (　　　) and more than the seven (　　　) (　　　) combined.

English Composition

次の日本文を英文に直してください．

1. 最近，VOA は米国における郡の重要性について報告した．（report を使って）

   _____

2. 全国には 3,000 を超える郡がある．（there を使って）

   _____

3. 国勢調査局は，2010 年から 2015 年の間に 1,653 の郡が，人口が減ったと報告している．（lost population を使って）

   _____

ひとくちコラム

　米国には本課題で話題になった深刻な過疎化を招いている郡があり，今後その対策も立てられると思われる．ところが，米国の全人口は毎年増加している．ジェトロの調査によると，消費規模で見ると「世界一の市場」である．米国の消費市場は毎年の人口増加により拡大傾向となっている．米国の移民政策と高い出生率で，人口は1967年には2億人を超え，現在3億人を超えている．2043年頃には4億人を突破するとみられている．市場規模や購買力では米国市場が世界一である．米国の経済力は，この人口増加から生み出されたものであるともいえる．

参考資料：ジェトロ「米国市場調査レポート」『ジェトロ』(https://www.jetro.go.jp/ext_images/jfile/report/07001419/1.pdf)

Unit 12 Racial and Ethnic Issue

Should Offensive Place Names Be Changed?

http://learningenglish.voanews.com/a/should-insensitive-place-names-be-changed/3370802.html

Should Offensive Place Names Be Changed?
出典：Public domain Pixabay under Creative Commons CC0
https://pixabay.com/ja/

00:00-05:31

1   Hundreds of places across the U.S. use the word "squaw," including Squaw Creek, Squaw Flat, Squaw Meadows and Squaw Springs, for example. In 1960, the Winter Olympics took place in a ski area called Squaw Valley, California.

But some people find the word offensive. It is an old word for an American Indian woman or wife. Many dictionaries note that the word is considered insulting. Few people use it in conversation anymore.

Now, some lawmakers and volunteers are trying to change place names that include the word "squaw," and other demeaning words, with names that are currently more acceptable.

A history of racial and ethnic insults

Place names such as Squaw Valley are historic, but they are also signs of a time when racial and ethnic insults were a common part of American society.

Other places that include racial and ethnic labels are "Negro Ben Mountain," "Jew Valley," "Chinaman's Hat," and "Redman Creek."

VOA generally does not broadcast these names or other, more-offensive names, or put them on our website, unless they are part of a news story. But many people continue to use these names. And they often still appear on maps and signs.

Lawmakers in six states have already approved bills to force or suggest changing controversial place names in their states. Committees must decide whether to keep a historical name even if some people may be insulted by it.

More than 30 offensive names

The state of Washington, in the northwest corner of the United States, is one of the places that is considering its place names carefully.

Pramila Jayapal is a Washington state senator. She convinced Washington's Department of Natural Resources to create a list of insulting place names. She then published the department's report.

The agency found 36 names. They include "Jim Crow Point" and "Jim Crow Creek."

In American English, the name "Jim Crow" was originally an insulting term for a black man. The term came to be used to describe laws that enforced racial separation in the United States from the 1870s -- after the Civil War -- to the 1950s and 1960s, when federal civil rights laws were passed that banned racial segregation.

Some people believe "Jim Crow Point" and "Jim Crow Creek" were named for a black man who deserted from the Navy and settled in the area in the 19th century.

But some area residents have different beliefs. One source says the name comes from a kind of bird -- called crows -- that lived in trees near a local river.

Another person who lives nearby, Joe Budnick, says Jim Crow Point and Jim Crow Creek were named after an Indian chief.

Budnick is a retired fisherman and truck driver. He says local people did not like state officials telling them to make changes to local place names.

"The inference was that we were racists and that we were stupid and didn't know we were offending people and all this other stuff -- when we're not," he complained.

Despite his objections to the political pressure, Budnick suggested some alternative names. He says Jim Crow Point could be named Brookfield Point because a town called Brookfield once existed in the area.

And, he says Jim Crow Creek could be named Harlows Creek, and Jim Crow Hill could be named Beare Hill, to honor a family that settled in the area long ago.

The state committee that reviews name suggestions liked Budnick's ideas. Committee members approved them for final consideration.

読解のための語彙，文法および構文

p.56 ℓ.1	hundreds of places across the U.S.:	米国内の何百もの場所
p.56 ℓ.1	squaw:	アメリカ先住民の女性または妻に関する古い言い方
p.56 ℓ.3	Winter Olympics took place:	冬季オリンピックが開催された．
p.56 ℓ.4	offensive:	不快な
p.56 ℓ.4	American Indian woman or wife:	アメリカ先住民の女性または妻
p.56 ℓ.6	in conversation:	会話で．
p.56 ℓ.7	lawmakers:	議員
p.56 ℓ.7	volunteers:	ボランティア
p.56 ℓ.8	demeaning words:	侮辱的な言葉
p.56 ℓ.10	racial and ethnic insults:	人種や民族に対する侮辱
p.56 ℓ.12	a common part of American society:	アメリカ社会の共通部分．
p.56 ℓ.15	more-offensive names:	より攻撃的な名前，
p.57 ℓ.19	controversial place names:	論争の的になっている地名
p.57 ℓ.19	committees:	委員会
p.57 ℓ.21	more than 30:	30 を超える．通常 more than A は A を含まないことに注意．
p.57 ℓ.24	a Washington state senator:	ワシントン州上院議員
p.57 ℓ.24	convince:	説得する
p.57 ℓ.24	Washington's Department of Natural Resources:	天然資源省のワシントン州支局
p.57 ℓ.29	originally an insulting term:	もともとは侮辱的な用語だった
p.57 ℓ.31	Civil War:	南北戦争
p.57 ℓ.32	racial segregation:	人種差別．
p.57 ℓ.35	deserted from the Navy:	海軍から脱走した．
p.57 ℓ.36	the name comes from 〜:	〜にちなんだ名前
p.57 ℓ.37	local river:	地元の川
p.57 ℓ.39	Indian chief:	先住民の首長
p.57 ℓ.42	inference:	推測
p.57 ℓ.43	complain:	苦情を言う，苦言を呈する
p.57 ℓ.44	despite:	〜だが，にもかかわらず
p.57 ℓ.44	suggested some alternative names:	代替名を提案した
p.57 ℓ.48	to honor 〜:	〜を称えるために
p.57 ℓ.48	settled in the area:	定住した

Reading Comprehension Questions

次の各文が，本文の内容に合っていればTを，合っていない場合はFを，括弧内に記入してください．

1. (　　) In 1960, the Winter Olympics took place in a ski area called Squaw Valley, California.
2. (　　) Now, some lawmakers and volunteers are nottrying to change place names that include the word "squaw," and other demeaning words, with names that are currently more acceptable.
3. (　　) VOA generally does not broadcast these names or other, more-offensive names, or put them on our website, unless they are part of a news story.
4. (　　) The state of Washington, in the northwest corner of the United States, is one of the places that is considering its place names carefully.
5. (　　) In British English, the name "Jim Crow" was originally an insulting term for a black man.
6. (　　) Some people believe "Jim Crow Point" and "Jim Crow Creek" were named for a black man who deserted from the Navy and settled in the area in the 18th century.
7. (　　) But some area residents have different beliefs. One source says the name comes from a kind of bird -- called crows -- that lived in trees near a local river.
8. (　　) Another person who lives nearby, Joe Budnick, says Jim Crow Point and Jim Crow Creek were named after an Indian chief.
9. (　　) Budnick is a retired fisherman and taxi driver.
10. (　　) The state committee that reviews name suggestions did not like Budnick's ideas.

Listening Comprehension Questions

次の英語を聴いて空欄を埋めてください．

http://learningenglish.voanews.com/pp/3370881/ppt0.html

(05:57-06:20)

Jon Shannon (　　　　) on one of the (　　　　). He (　　　) he would never (　　　　) someone a "squaw." But, he (　　　　), "there is a difference between (　　) it personal and the history that (　　) along with the place names that (　　) (　　) (　　) historically. I (　　) I just don't see anything wrong with that."

English Composition

次の日本文を英文に直してください．

1. スコー・バレーのような地名は歴史的だが，人種や民族に対する侮辱がアメリカ社会の共通部分だった時代の名残でもある．（a common part of を使って）

2. 委員会は，たとえその名前によって侮辱される人々がいても歴史的な名前を残すことが許容できるか否かを決定しなければならない．（even if を使って）

3. 委員会委員は最終審査の際，その名前を承認した．（final consideration を使って）

ひとくちコラム

　アファーマティブアクションとは，米国で企業や団体，学校が，人種，出身国，性別等が理由で雇用や教育上の差別を行わない．また，差別を受けてきた黒人（アフリカ系アメリカ人）等少数民族の人々，女性の社会的地位向上に向けて雇用や教育に関して積極的に優遇措置をとることをアファーマティブアクションという．さらに米国政府の政策や裁判所命令で企業等に対し，そうした措置を義務づけることをさしている．米国ではこうした動きが多く，大学などでも少数民族の志願者に対し優遇措置が取られている．ただし，少数民族や女性を採用，昇進において優遇するのは逆差別という批判もある．今回の記事の話題も差別を受けてきた少数民族に関するその土地の歴史的背景を調べた上で慎重な検討が必要であろう．

参考資料：国立国会図書館「レファレンス事例詳細」『国立国会図書館』
　　　　　〈http://crd.ndl.go.jp/reference/modules/d3ndlcrdentry/index.php?page=ref_view&id=1000115507〉

Unit 13

Religion

One in Four Married Americans Do Not Share Same Religion as Wife, Husband

http://learningenglish.voanews.com/a/one-quarter-married-americans-do-not-share-same-religion-as-wife-husband-pew-/3573197.html

出典：Public domain Pixabay under Creative Commons CC0
https://pixabay.com/ja/

[00:00-03:59]

Twenty-five percent of married adults in the United States have different religious beliefs than their husband or wife.

That could be a Christian mother and a Jewish father, or a very religious mother and a father who is not religious.

This information comes from the Pew Research Center, an independent research group in Washington, D.C. The center based its findings on a 2014 opinion survey of 35,000 Americans.

Mother Knows Best

Children raised in homes with parents of different religious beliefs were most influenced by their mothers, Pew found.

Forty-eight percent raised in mixed religion homes identified with their mother's religion, the center reported. Only 28 percent identified with their father's religion.

Nearly one in four people from a mixed religious home did not identify with either of their parents' religious beliefs.

How Important is Shared Religious Beliefs?

People surveyed by Pew were asked about how important it was to them to share the same religious beliefs with their spouse.

Forty-four percent said sharing the same religious beliefs is very important to a successful marriage. But that is not as high as the percentages of Americans who found other reasons important, Pew said.

A bigger percentage, over 60 percent, found shared interests, a satisfying sexual relationship and sharing household duties as very important to a successful marriage.

Forty-six percent said having enough money is very important to a successful marriage. That was higher than the percentage who identified shared religious beliefs as very important.

Sixty-two percent of people married to someone of the same religion said this was a very or somewhat important to their decision to marry that person.

Eighty-four percent of people who do not identify with a religion said the religious beliefs of their spouse were not important in their decision to marry.

The center said the number of Americans raised in homes with people who do not share the same religious beliefs is growing.

Pew reported that 39 percent of people who have been married since 2010 have a spouse with different religious beliefs.

Only 19 percent of those who married before 1960 were married to a person of a different religion, Pew said.

The religious make-up of Americans is also changing, according to Pew.

Christianity is still the major religion in the United States. Over 70 percent of people surveyed by Pew described themselves as Christian in 2014. But that is down from 78.4 percent in 2007.

About 1.9 percent of Americans described themselves as Jewish, up from 1.7 percent in 2007. Muslims make up 0.9 percent of the population, up from 0.4 percent in 2007, Pew said.

Nearly 22.8 percent of Americans said in 2014 that they are not connected to any religion, up from 16.1 percent in 2007. These can be people who do not believe in organized religion, or those who believe in the idea of a God, but not in any one religion.

Unit 13 One in Four Married Americans Do Not Share Same Religion as Wife, Husband 63

読解のための語彙，文法および構文

p.61 ℓ.1	twenty-five percent of:	の25%
p.61 ℓ.1	married adults:	結婚した成人
p.61 ℓ.2	religious beliefs:	宗教的信仰
p.61 ℓ.3	Christian:	キリスト教徒
p.61 ℓ.3	Jewish:	ユダヤ教徒
p.61 ℓ.6	based:	基づいた
p.61 ℓ.6	opinion survey:	意見調査
p.61 ℓ.9	raised in homes with parents of different religious beliefs:	両親が異なる宗教的信仰を持つ家庭で育った
p.61 ℓ.9	most influenced by:	最も影響を受ける
p.61 ℓ.11	identified with:	「確認される」「特定される」などの訳があるが，ここは「信仰を持つ」などと訳すと分かりやすい．
p.61 ℓ.13	nearly one in four people:	およそ4人に1人
p.62 ℓ.16	people surveyed by Pew:	「ピュー・センターが調査した人々」と訳すと分かりやすい．
p.62 ℓ.16	were asked about〜:	「〜について質問を受けた」と能動態で訳すと文章が分かりやすい．
p.62 ℓ.18	sharing the same religious beliefs:	同じ宗教的信仰を共有すること
p.62 ℓ.19	a successful marriage:	成功する結婚
p.62 ℓ.21	shared interests, a satisfying sexual relationship and sharing household duties:	興味の共有，満足のいく性的関係，家事の分担
p.62 ℓ.28	somewhat:	ある程度
p.62 ℓ.30	spouse:	配偶者
p.62 ℓ.30	decision to marry:	結婚の決定
p.62 ℓ.31	the number of Americans:	米国人の数
p.62 ℓ.35	only 19 percent:	19%にすぎない
p.62 ℓ.37	the religious make-up of Americans:	米国人の宗教的構成
p.62 ℓ.37	according to Pew:	ピュー・センターによると
p.62 ℓ.38	Christianity:	キリスト教
p.62 ℓ.38	still:	依然として
p.62 ℓ.38	the major religion:	主要な宗教
p.62 ℓ.39	that is down from 78.4 percent:	78.4%から下がっている
p.62 ℓ.41	described themselves as Jewish:	自分はユダヤ人であると述べている
p.62 ℓ.44	nearly 22.8 percent of Americans:	米国人の22.8%が

p.62 ℓ.44　not connected to any religion: どの宗教も信仰していない
p.62 ℓ.45　up from 16.1 percent in 2007: 2007年の16.1％から上昇している
p.62 ℓ.46　organized religion: 組織化された宗教
p.62 ℓ.46　believe in: 信じる
p.62 ℓ.46　the idea of a God: 神の教え

Reading Comprehension Questions

次の各文が，本文の内容に合っていればTを，合っていない場合はFを，括弧内に記入してください．

1. (　) Twenty-five percent of married adults in the United States have different religious beliefs than their husband or wife.
2. (　) The center based its findings on a 2016 opinion survey of 350,000 Americans.
3. (　) Forty-eight percent raised in mixed religion homes identified with their father's religion, the center reported.
4. (　) Nearly one in four people from a mixed religious home did not identify with either of their parents' religious beliefs.
5. (　) Forty-four percent said sharing the same religious beliefs is very important to a successful marriage.
6. (　) Forty-six percent said having enough money is not very important to a successful marriage.
7. (　) Eighty-four percent of people who do not identify with a religion said the religious beliefs of their spouse were not important in their decision to marry.
8. (　) Pew reported that 39 percent of people who have been married since 2010 have a spouse with different religious beliefs.
9. (　) Christianity is still the major religion in the United States.
10. (　) Nearly 22.8 percent of Americans said in 2016 that they are not connected to any religion, up from 16.1 percent in 2005.

Listening Comprehension Questions

次の英語を聴いて空欄を埋めてください.

http://learningenglish.voanews.com/pp/3573493/ppt0.html

[00:10-00:34]

(　　　) (　　) of married adults in the United States (　　　) different religious beliefs than their husband or wife.

That (　　) (　　) a Christian mother and a Jewish father, or a very religious mother and a father who is not (　　　).

This information (　　) (　　) the Pew Research Center, an (　　　) research group in Washington, D.C. The center (　　) its findings on a 2014 opinion survey of 35,000 Americans.

English Composition

次の日本文を英文に直してください.

1. 異なる宗教的信仰を持つ両親の家庭で育った子ども達は，母親の影響を最も受けることが判明した．(most influenced by を使って)

2. 回答者の44％が成功する結婚には同じ宗教的信仰を共有することが非常に重要だと述べた．(is very important to を使って)

3. キリスト教は依然として米国の主要な宗教である．(still を使って)

> **ひとくちコラム**
>
> 　内閣府経済社会総合研究所によると，アメリカの出生力の高さはアメリカ人の信仰心の強さが原因となっている．ただし，どう研究所は夫婦間で異なる宗教を持つか否かには言及していない．アメリカは伝統的にプロテスタント社会であるが，カトリックを信仰する中南米からの移民や中東からの移民の増加，無宗教人口の増加で，プロテスタント人口は半数を上回る程度になった．2002年の調査では，総人口に占める割合は，プロテスタントが55%，ローマ・カトリックが22%，その他が13%，無宗教人口が11%になっている．こうした宗教の混在が記事にあるような夫婦間の宗教の違いにも影響を及ぼすと考えられる．アメリカは人種のるつぼといわれる国であり，宗教においても近年は多様性のある国であると言えよう．
>
> 参考資料：是川夕，岩澤美帆「増え続ける米国人口とその要因：人種・エスニシティ・宗教における多様性」『内閣府経済社会総合研究所』(2009) (http://www.esri.go.jp/jp/archive/e_dis/e_dis226/e_dis226.pdf)

Unit 14　　　　　　　　　　　　　US Pop Culture

Winans: Music, God and Family

http://learningenglish.voanews.com/a/people-in-america-bebe-winans/3446109.html

出典：VOA, Public Domain
http://gdb.voanews.com/2B51C7C1-0382-4BE5-B82D-
D34A1287D331_w610_r1_s.jpg

(00:17-05:55)

1　　That is the voice of singer and songwriter BeBe Winans. His birth name is Benjamin but he is known to all as "BeBe."

　　BeBe comes from a large Christian family. His parents, Delores and David Winans, raised seven sons and three daughters.

5　　Winans says music, God and family were the foundation of his upbringing.

　　"Growing up in the family I grew up in, evolved around music, it evolved around God and it evolved around family. When we went to church, it was family and it is the main foundation, I think, I've had since I've left home, since I've left Detroit, Michigan."

10　　At the age of 17, BeBe and his 15-year old sister Priscilla, called CeCe, left home for Pineville, North Carolina. They began their professional music careers as background singers on the popular Christian television show "PTL Club." PTL stood for Praise the Lord.

　　Winans says the hosts of the show, Jim and Tammy Faye Bakker, treated him
15　and his sister as family. While there, the siblings recorded their first album, "Lord Lift Us Up," for PTL Records.

In 1987, the Winans left "PTL Club." That same year they released their first album, "BeBe & CeCe Winans." The mainstream album gave them their first R & B hit, "I.O.U. Me."

The brother and sister recorded five albums together. In 1995, they decided to seek individual careers.

As a lyricist, BeBe Winans says he always knew he could express his spirituality in any song -- be it gospel or contemporary.

"I think what separated me in my writing with others is that I felt that I could talk about what God meant to me in every area of my life...in my relationships, in my family and in my work, in everything, in play, in every aspect of my life. So I was moved by songs that wasn't in the gospel category all my life. So, 'Coming Back Home,' and 'Love Said Not So' and 'Lost Without You' and 'In The Meantime,' you know, all those songs is reflective of my life."

BeBe Winans has several solo albums and six Grammy awards. He also has written and produced hit songs for others. And he is an actor and author.

His latest professional undertaking is a musical about his life. Winans and family friend and director Charles Randolph-Wright together wrote "Born for This, The BeBe Winans Story."

The artist says it all began with a phone conversation with the singer-songwriter Roberta Flack.

"The musical started with a phone call. And that was a phone call with Roberta Flack. And we were talking about everything other than the musical, and right in the middle of the conversation she detoured and said, 'BeBe, when are you going to write that musical about you and your family?' It's an American musical, it's a story, it's a film after that, and four days later, I'm at a hotel in Montreal. I walk in and I open up my laptop and it was like a faucet came on. And right then and there, I wrote the first draft of what now is 'Born for This.'"

読解のための語彙，文法および構文

p.67 ℓ.1　the voice of: の歌声

p.67 ℓ.1　singer and songwriter BeBe Winans: シンガーソングライターのビービー・ワイナンズ

p.67 ℓ.1　birth name: 出生時の名前

p.67 ℓ.3　come from ～ : ～出身

p.67 ℓ.3	**a large Christian family:** キリスト教徒の大家族	
p.67 ℓ.5	**foundation:** 基盤	
p.67 ℓ.5	**upbringing:** 養育	
p.67 ℓ.6	**growing up in the family:** 家族の中で成長する	
p.67 ℓ.6	**evolved around ～:** ～を軸に展開する．（この箇所は文脈に即して訳す）	
p.67 ℓ.8	**left home:** 家を出る	
p.67 ℓ.10	**at the age of 17:** 17歳のとき	
p.67 ℓ.11	**left home for Pineville, North Carolina:** ノースカロライナ州パインビルに向かうため家を出た	
p.67 ℓ.11	**began their professional music careers as background singers:** バックコーラスの歌手としてプロのキャリアを歩み始めた．	
p.67 ℓ.13	**PTL stood for Praise the Lord:** PTLは神である主を賛美する番組だった	
p.67 ℓ.14	**the hosts of the show:** ショーの主催者	
p.67 ℓ.14	**treated him and his sister as family:** 彼と妹を家族として扱った	
p.68 ℓ.17	**released their first album, "BeBe & CeCe Winans":** 最初のアルバム「ビービー＆セス・ワイナンズ」をリリースした	
p.68 ℓ.21	**individual careers:** ソロとしてのキャリア	
p.68 ℓ.22	**lyricist:** 作詞家	
p.68 ℓ.23	**spirituality:** 精神性	
p.68 ℓ.23	**gospel:** ゴスペル	
p.68 ℓ.23	**contemporary:** コンテンポラリー	
p.68 ℓ.25	**relationships:** 関係性	
p.68 ℓ.27	**moved by songs:** 歌に感動する	
p.68 ℓ.27	**'Coming Back Home,':** 「家路につく」	
p.68 ℓ.28	**'Love Said Not So':** 「愛してはいない」	
p.68 ℓ.28	**'Lost Without You':** 「君無しではいられない」	
p.68 ℓ.28	**'In The Meantime,':** 「合間に」	
p.68 ℓ.30	**Grammy awards:** グラミー賞	
p.68 ℓ.33	**Charles Randolph-Wright:** チャールズ・ランドルフ・ライト	
p.68 ℓ.34	**"Born for This, The BeBe Winans Story":** 「このために生まれた．ビービー・ワイナンズ物語」	
p.68 ℓ.35	**artist:** アーティスト	
p.68 ℓ.36	**Roberta Flack:** ロバータ・フラック	
p.68 ℓ.40	**American musical:** アメリカ人のミュージカル	

Reading Comprehension Questions

次の各文が，本文の内容に合っていればTを，合っていない場合はFを，括弧内に記入してください．

1. (　　) BeBe Winans' birth name is Benjamin but he is known to all as "BeBe."
2. (　　) His parents, Delores and David Winans, raised three sons and seven daughters.
3. (　　) At the age of 18, BeBe and his 17-year old sister Priscilla, called CeCe, left home for Pineville, North Carolina.
4. (　　) In 1987, the Winans left "PTL Club."
5. (　　) As a lyricist, BeBe Winans says he always knew he could not express his spirituality in any song.
6. (　　) BeBe Winans has several solo albums and six Grammy awards.
7. (　　) BeBe has written and produced hit songs only for himself.
8. (　　) His latest professional undertaking is a musical about his life.
9. (　　) The artist says it all began with a phone conversation with the singer-songwriter Roberta Flack.
10. (　　) Bebe and Roberta Flack were talking about everything including the musical at first on the phone.

Listening Comprehension Questions

次の英語を聴いて空欄を埋めてください．

http://learningenglish.voanews.com/audio/audio/348402.html

06:05-06:38

It (　　　) (　　　) coming of age of two young (　　　) (　　　) being thrust from a (　　　) up until that point of predominantly a (　　　) situation and then thrust into a world that was predominantly a white situation. So we endured racism, we endured a lot of things, but just a (　　　) (　　　), you know. (　　　) worlds, you know. It talks about (　　　) myself.

English Composition

次の日本文を英文に直してください．

1. ワイナンズは，音楽，神と家族は自分を養育してくれた基盤だと述べている．(the foundation of を使って)

2. 兄と妹は5枚のアルバムをともに録音した．（record を使って）

3. ビービー・ワイナンズは複数のソロアルバムをリリースし，6回グラミー賞受賞経験がある．（have を使って）

> **ひとくちコラム**
>
> 　ビービー・ワイナンズはゴスペル音楽で活躍しているワイナンズ一家の1人である．ゴスペルソングは神を称える賛美歌として知られている．賛美歌というと厳かで静かな歌を思い浮かべる人が多いかもしれないが，ゴスペルソングは，アメリカでは手拍子があったり，足踏みがあったりと動きがある賛美の歌が多い．1993年にウーピー・ゴールドバーグが主演した『天使にラブソングを』の映画は世界的にヒットした．この中で歌われていたゴスペルソングは今でもよく歌われている．

復習用　ミニ TOEIC テスト 2 回分

Test 1

Listening test

Part 1

　Directions: For each question, you will hear four statements about a photo in your test book. After listening to the statements, please select the one that best describes what you see in the photo.

1. Look at picture number 1 in your test book.

　　Mark your answer. (A) (B) (C) (D)

Part 2

　Directions: You will hear a statement or question and three answers in English. They are printed on your test book and will be played once. Please select the best answer to the statement or question.

2. Mark your answer. (A) (B) (C)

3. Mark your answer. (A) (B) (C)

Part 3

　Directions: You will hear conversations between two or more people. The conversations are not printed in your test sheet and will be played once. You will be asked three questions about what the speakers discuss in each conversation. Please select the best answer to each question.

　Questions 4 through 6 are related to the following conversation.

4. Where is the conversation taking place?

   (A) At a bus terminal.

   (B) At a car rental agency.

   (C) At a train station.

   (D) At an airport.

   Mark your answer. (A) (B) (C) (D)

5. What does staff C suggests the questioner do?

   (A) Talk in the lobby.

   (B) Call a taxi agent.

   (C) Look at a bus schedule.

   (D) Drop her baggage.

   Mark your answer. (A) (B) (C) (D)

6. Where will the questioner probably go next?

   (A) To a ticket machine.

   (B) To a department store.

   (C) To a telephone booth.

   (D) To a souvenir shop.

   Mark your answer. (A) (B) (C) (D)

Part 4

Directions:

You will listen to a single person speaking. You will be asked three questions about what the speaker says. Please select the best answer to each question. The dialogue is not printed in your test sheet and will only be played once.

Questions 7 through 9 concern the following text.

7. What is the announcement mainly about?

   (A) A new store.

   (B) A music school project.

   (C) A new arts center.

   (D) Local community members.

   Mark your answer. (A) (B) (C) (D)

8. Who is George Johnson?

(A) A singer.

(B) A governor.

(C) An architect.

(D) A teacher.

Mark your answer. (A) (B) (C) (D)

9. According to the speaker, what will happen in November?

(A) A policy will go into effect.

(B) Tickets will go on sale.

(C) A show will be performed.

(D) A lecture will start.

Mark your answer. (A) (B) (C) (D)

This is end of the listening test.

Reading test

You will read various texts and answers related questions.

Part 5

Directions: A word or phrase is missing in each sentence. Select the best answer to complete the sentence.

10. Factory tests ____ helped Asix Company to improve the design of its popular dress.

(A) has

(B) have

(C) has been

(D) had being

Mark your answer. (A) (B) (C) (D)

11. Any mechanical malfunction equipment should ____ reported to the manager immediately.

(A) be

(B) been

(C) being

(D) have

Mark your answer. (A) (B) (C) (D)

Part 6

Directions: Read the following texts. A sentence, phrase or word is missing in each text. Select the best answer to complete the sentence.

Questions 12-13 refer to the following notice.

Training for Sales Staff

Delaware Publishing is committed to the success and productivity of its entire sales staff and we would like to hear 12. _____ you. The training office at Delaware Publishing has put together a schedule of workshops on computer skills and sales techniques for the next year. We invite your suggestions for topics that you imagine would 13. _____ you in the performance of your current job responsibilities.

12. (A) on
    (B) from
    (C) at
    (D) in
    Mark your answer. (A) (B) (C) (D)

13. (A) suggest
    (B) advantage
    (C) benefit
    (D) react
    Mark your answer. (A) (B) (C) (D)

Part 7

Directions: You will read a selection of texts, including e-mails, magazine and newspaper articles, and advertisement messages. Several questions follow the texts. Please select the best answer.

Questions 14 and 15 refer to the following texts.

Fabric Manufacturers Exhibition

Blue River Hotel, 65 Cherry Street, Goldtown, N.C.27211.
Event Schedule: Friday, March 25.

Keynote Talk, by Nancy Smith, 8:30-9:30 a.m., Main Exhibition Room.
The president of the Fabric Manufacturers Association will welcome attendees to the conference.

Fashion Trend Prediction of Designers, by Anne Holding, 9:30-10:30 a.m., Stefan Room.

The speaker will discuss upcoming trends in fabrics for casual women's clothing.

New Ways in Clothing Design, by Peter Keller, 10:30-11:30 a.m., Samuel Room.

The speaker will examine how designers use fabric to create shape and movement in their clothes.

Displays, 1:00-5:30 p.m., Exhibitors Hall.

Over 40 fabric manufacturers will exhibit samples of their latest fabrics.

Fashion Show conducted by Nancy Smith, 5:30-8:00 p.m., Hotel Atrium.

Please enjoy the collection of five active fashion designers using the most popular fabrics.

14. Who is Ms. Smith?

    (A) An association president.

    (B) An emerging fashion designer.

    (C) A clothing store owner.

    (D) A hotel manager.

    Mark your answer. (A) (B) (C) (D)

15. Where will the fashion show take place?

    (A) In the main exhibition room.

    (B) In the Stefan Room.

    (C) In the Exhibitors hall.

    (D) In the hotel atrium.

    Mark your answer. (A) (B) (C) (D)

Questions 16 and 17 refer to the following texts.

WELCOME TO UNION STREET STATIONERY

HOME   PRODUCTSPLACE ORDER   FEEDBACK

Contact Information

Customer service representatives are available to help you by telephone from Monday to Friday, 8 A.M. to 6 P.M.

Phone: 0845 555 0102

Phone: (outside UK) : +44 (0) 131 555 1001

Email: service@unionstreetstationery.com

(Our representatives respond to most inquiries within 48 hours.)

Mailing address: Union Street Stationery, Concordia 21, South Street Portstyle Brighton BN40 1DH

Shipping

Product orders of products usually are usually shipped within three business days. However, specially designed products require a processing time of seven to ten business days prior to shipping.

Shipping from our supply center in Edinburgh takes two to four days. Orders shipped to overseas destinations usually arrive in two to three weeks.

16. For whom is the information provided?

    (A) Customers ordering products.

    (B) Employees responding to requests.

    (C) Mail workers sending packages.

    (D) Company printing stationery.

    Mark your answer. (A) (B) (C) (D)

17. What is described on the Web page?

    (A) Custom orders are not accepted.

    (B) E-mail inquiries are not recommended.

    (C) International orders are available.

    (D) All products are shipped within two days.

    Mark your answer. (A) (B) (C) (D)

Test 2

Listening test

Part 1

Directions: For each question, you will hear four statements about a photo in your test book. After listening the statements, please select one that best describes what you see in the photo.

1. Look at picture number 1 in your test book.

Mark your answer. (A) (B) (C) (D)

Part 2

Directions: You will hear a statement or question and three answers in English. They are printed on your test sheet and will be played once. Please select the best answer to the statement or question.

2. Mark your answer. (A) (B) (C)
3. Mark your answer. (A) (B) (C)

Part 3

Directions: You will hear conversations between two or more people. The conversations are not printed in your test sheet and will be played once. You will be asked three questions about what the speakers discuss in each conversation. Please select the best answer to each question. Questions 4 through 6 are related to the following conversation.

4. What is the conversation mainly about?

(A) An enlargement of office room.

(B) A change of company owner.

(C) A decrease in employees.

(D) An entry into a new market.

Mark your answer. (A) (B) (C) (D)

5. Why does the second person say, "It's incredible!"?

(A) She strongly opposes the news.

(B) She wants to explain the news.

(C) She is disappointed.

(D) She is happily surprised.

Mark your answer. (A) (B) (C) (D)

6. What do the speakers imply about the company?

(A) It has an old building.

(B) It is planning to add salaries.

(C) It is in a good financial situation.

(D) It has many offices in the country.

Mark your answer. (A) (B) (C) (D)

Part 4

Directions: You will hear a single person speaking. You will be asked three questions about what the speaker says. Please select the best answer to each question from (A), (B), (C) or (D). The conversations are not printed in your test sheet and are spoken once.

Questions 7 through 9 are related to the following conversation.

7. What type of products does the shop sell?
   (A) Jewelry and cosmetics.
   (B) Fruits and vegetables.
   (C) Stationary and clothes.
   (D) Baked goods and drinks.
   Mark your answer. (A) (B) (C) (D)

8. What did product journal say about Freund Bakery's products?
   (A) The graham bread is the most popular product.
   (B) They are more affordable than products found at similar bakeries.
   (C) They are very popular this season.
   (D) They are made from natural ingredients.
   Mark your answer. (A) (B) (C) (D)

9. When does the promotion end?
   (A) On Friday.
   (B) On Saturday.
   (C) On Sunday.
   (D) On Monday.
   Mark your answer. (A) (B) (C) (D)

This is end of the listening test.

Part 5

Directions: A word or phrase is missing in each sentence. Select the best answer to complete the sentence.

10. The preparation of the materials must _____ by the end of this week at any cost.
    (A) complete
    (B) been completed
    (C) being completed

(D) be completed

Mark your answer. (A) (B) (C) (D)

11. Bill Johnson needs to ____ the report by the end of this month. Other managers will expect his punctuality.

(A) have revised

(B) been revised

(C) being revised

(D) revise

Mark your answer. (A) (B) (C) (D)

Part 6

Read the following texts. A sentence, phrase or word is missing in each text. Select the best answer to complete the sentence from four answer choices and mark the letter (A), (B), (C), or (D).

Questions 12-13 refer to the following letter.

February 25

Ms. Jeng Fu

200 Queen Street

Kingston, ON 01123

Dear Ms. Fu:

We appreciate for your order. 12. ____ we have already shipped most of your items, the Desk Top Computer (LAN 025) is currently out of stock. We are contacting our suppliers regarding your order, but the product is not likely to be available for a few days. We would be happy to substitute a similar item of your selection, or we can 13. ____ your payment for this product.

We are sorry for the inconvenience. Please contact our order department at 77-1603-3901 for further information.

Love White

Manager, Green Electronics, Inc.

12. (A) Despite

(B) And

(C) However

(D) Although

Mark your answer. (A) (B) (C) (D)

13. (A) have been refunding

(B) refund

(C) have refunded

(D) be refunded

Mark your answer. (A) (B) (C) (D)

Part 7

Directions: You will read a selection of texts, including e-mails, magazine and newspaper articles, and advertisement messages. Several questions follow the texts. Please select the best answer to each question.

Questions 14 through 15 refer to the following texts.

Peachtree Press

111 Peachtree Street NE

Suite 400 – West Building

Atlanta, GA 30303

www.peachtreepress.com

September 25

Mr. John Thomas, 1999 SW 5th Ave #100, Portland, OR 97204

Dear Mr. Thomas:

We at Peachtree Press are pleased that you have accepted to work with us again on an update and additional printing of your book "Global Tour: A Tourist's Guide." Rest assured that we understand the ongoing dramatic transformation in our field and are very glad that we can renew your previous contract with us to understand such a paradigm shift. -(1)- Since the original "Global Tour" received such a good reception in the target markets, we would like to make sure that the renewed version meets the needs of both existing and new readers. The new version will also be published in the form of an electronic book so it can be more easily distributed and bring in various potential audiences. -(2)- All provisions of the previous contract will remain unchanged, except for the renewal of your royalty fees as we consulted with you prior.

-(3)- The renewed agreement is enclosed. If you agree to it, please sign with your full name and date it. I appreciate it if you could return it to us by October 10. -(4)-

Thank you for attending to this matter in a timely manner and your wonderful contributions to the world of travel books. We respect our authors and are especially honored to work with you. Please do not hesitate to let us know if you have any questions.

Sincerely,

Catherine Carpenter

Director, Peachtree Press

14. Why did Ms. Carpenter send the letter to Mr. Thomas?

    (A) To ask him to review a book.

    (B) To inquire about a travel schedule.

    (C) To examine that he can sign books.

    (D) To explain a modification to an agreement.

    Mark your answer.　(A)　(B)　(C)　(D)

15. The wording "attending to" in line 1, paragraph 3, is closest in meaning to

    (A) planning to go to

    (B) discovering of

    (C) taking care of

    (D) being present at

    Mark your answer.　(A)　(B)　(C)　(D)

16. What did Ms. Carpenter send with the letter?

    (A) A revised contract.

    (B) A writer information.

    (C) A copy of a book.

    (D) A book review.

    Mark your answer.　(A)　(B)　(C)　(D)

17. In which of the positions （1）, （2）, （3）, and （4） does the following sentence belong?

    "A new chapter about traveling in Southeast Asia will be sure to attract new attention."

    (A) (1)

    (B) (2)

    (C) (3)

    (D) (4)

    Mark your answer.　(A)　(B)　(C)　(D)

Questions 18 through 20 refer to the following texts.

MEMO

Date: December 15

 We would like to inform you of William Stock's upcoming retirement. Mr. Stock started his 40-year career at the Earth Fund as a wildlife forest ranger in the Louisiana Wildlife Park. He has had five different positions, finally becoming the general director of conservation for all Louisiana Wildlife Parks. He has had this position for 10 years, leading with vision and commitment. Now at 65 years old, he is leaving us for a retirement.

 The Board of Directors has decided to send him a Lifetime Achievement Award with a commemorative medal at the staff meeting next Monday. Following the staff meeting, we will invite all employees to attend a party to honor Mr. Stock and his great contributions. If you want to write a goodbye to Mr. Stock, please come by Anthony Brown's office to write in the book that will be presented to him at the party.

18. In what field is Mr. Stock engaged in?

   (A) Senior education.

   (B) Archiving history.

   (C) Nature protection.

   (D) City development.

   Mark your answer. (A) (B) (C) (D)

19. What will NOT be given to honor Mr. Stock?

   (A) A medal.

   (B) An award.

   (C) A book.

   (D) A photo album.

   Mark your answer. (A) (B) (C) (D)

20. For how many years has Mr. Stock worked at the Earth Fund?

   (A) 10.

   (B) 15.

   (C) 40.

   (D) 65.

   Mark your answer. (A) (B) (C) (D)

訳例と解答

Unit 1. トラックが無人配送を初めて実現：ビール運送
【訳例】
　自動で運転をするトラックが，企業からの商品輸送を初めて行った．
　トラックは近年，コロラド州の西側で，バドワイザービールを大量に運んでいた．
　その車は，人間が運転をすることなく，190キロのほとんどを何の問題もなく移動した．
　ウーバーという，互いに運転を共有することで経営を行う企業があり，その一企業であるオットー社が，無人トラックを操作した．

高技術のビール運送経営
　トラックはおよそ5万缶ものビールを，フォートコリンズ市からコロラドスプリングスまで運搬した．
　その間，トラックは平均時速およそ89キロ毎時で，2時間走り続けた，とオットー社は述べた．
　会社が述べるには，熟練の運転手が移動の間にはトラック内にいたということであった．
　だが，その運転手は運転席に座りっぱなしになり，そのトラックの運転は，高速道路に出たり入ったりした時にのみ行った．
　それ以外の時間は，くつろいだり，寝たりするための，トラック内にある場所に座っていたという．

都市部用運転には向かない
　オットー社の自動運転技術は，高速道路での走行時のみに開発されたものである．
　こういった広い道路では，信号機や，道路を横切る歩行者などはいない．
　この技術は，部品やソフトウエアを含んで，およそ3万ドルを加算すれば，現存のトラックに搭載することができるのである．
　オットー社を共に創業した者はアンソニー・レバンドフスキーであり，彼はグーグル社における自動運転車の，前開発者である．
　彼が言うには，コンピューターが次の10年に行うであろう最も重要な行動は，人間のために車やトラックを運転するということである．
　彼の経営する会社は，安全に対して細心の注意を払っていることを，彼は付け加えた．
　オットー社の無人トラックを，道路で走らせることに抵抗感を感じる必要はない，ということをも述べている．
　「ソフトウエアの線路の上を走る列車のようなものです．」と，彼は説明する．
　「車内に人が誰も乗っていない車が走っているのを見ると，衝突することはないな，ということが，おわかりになられるでしょう．」
　アンホイザー・ブッシュ氏は，無人運転による配達をすることで，技術というものがいかに次代における輸送に対するすばらしい革新となっているか，といったことが示される，と述べた．

企業が計画していることは，自動運転を行うトラックを活用しながら，毎年120万本以上ものビールを運搬するということである．

　だが，無人運転を迎える将来的にも，人員は必要であるとのことである．無人の運転に限界がある場合や，積荷の過程を監視したり，運行全般の管理をする時に，人員は活用されるからである．

ブライアン・リン
　ブライアン・リンは，この逸話をロイター社からの報告や，関連会社からの報告を元に，VOAの英語用教材として執筆した．編集者はマリオ・リッターである．
　読者の方々からのご連絡をお待ち申し上げます．
　コメントもぜひお寄せ下さい．また，フェイスブックのページもご覧下さい．

【Reading Comprehension Questions 解答】
1. F 2. F 3. T 4. F 5. T 6. T 7. T 8. F 9. F 10. F

【Listening Comprehension Questions 解答】
Hello, listeners. My name is Bryan Lynn. Today, I'm going to talk about driverless (truck). The company Otto had a design of autonomous (technology). This is used only on (highways), because the truck without driving (operation) can move without taking care of traffic (signals) or pedestrians. In (addition), we can add the technology, including parts and software, to the (present) trucks with $30,000.

【English Composition 解答】
1. The most important thing government must do over the next ten years is revive economic action.
2. She added that her food company had been very concerned about safety for meals for a long time.
3. Delivery by motorcycle shows how bikes in a traffic jam in urban places are becoming the great innovation in transportation.

Unit 2. ジェンダー
【訳例】
　年は1913年．新しい大統領が選ばれ，まさに着任しようとしている．
　だが，その大統領がワシントンDCにある駅に到着した時には，出迎えに来た者はごくわずかである．
　「出迎えの者達はどこだ？」大統領は尋ねる．
　一向は既にペンシルバニア通りまで来ており，これまでにアメリカの大衆が経験したことのな

いものを見ることになる．それは，数千人もの女性で，通りを行進していたのだった．

彼女たちは何をしたいのか．それは選挙権を得ることである．

「米国憲法は1つ言い忘れていることがある．それは，前文で，選挙権を持っているのは誰であるか，ということである．

選挙権を持っている者で，権力のある者は皆，アメリカに居住することができるのである．」

ロビン・マンシーは，メリーランド大学・カレッジパークの歴史学を専門とする教授である．

マンシー教授が説明することには，アメリカの政治体系において，権限は連邦政府と州に振り分けられているということである．

「すなわち，19世紀後半における婦人参政権論者には参政権があったのである．

その婦人参政権論者は，連邦法案の改正を行おうとしているか，または州ごとに効力を発揮させることができたのである．そしてその州の中で，多くの場合において，女性は州レベルでより多くの権限を持っていたのである．」

女性はどちらの権限をも持つことを決めた．婦人参政権を獲得するための闘争が，19世紀から20世紀にかけて，連邦政府や各州で執り行われた．「Suffrage（参政権）」とは，選挙権を持つための権利のことを指す．

19世紀：各州における草の根作戦

当初は，参政権を求めていた女性はごくわずかばかりであった．

女性には男性と同じ価値があるものである．だから，女性も同じ政治的，立法的な権利があるべきである，と，女性たちは述べている．

こういった女性たちはアメリカを飛び回りながら，女性にも平等権を与えるように訴え，それぞれの街で条例を作成している人たちとも会合をしている．

だが，メリーランド州にあるゴーチャー大学の歴史家であるジーン・ベイカー氏は，彼女たちの考え方は，常に大衆からの指示を仰げるものではない，と述べている．

「女性たちは，自分たちの話が終わった後に，その追跡調査をされるような女性ならではの話がある．そして，夜を過ごすために自宅に戻っているのかもしれない．

そして，群集は，女性陣にあらゆる種類の腐った卵などを投げつけているのである．

だが，群集たちも多数派意見の反対に苦しんでいるのである．

当時，大部分の人たちは，その中には女性を含んでいるのであるが，選挙に参加をする女性などという者は自然ではない，と考えていた．

こういった群集は，男性と女性は，基本的には反対なのだ，と強く感じていた．

「男性というものは競争心が激しく，生まれつき高圧的なものなのだ．また，自己主張も強い．さらに，公的な生活をしているものであり，それがしみついているものなのだ．

一方，女性は，生まれつきおしとやかに，協調性を持ち，家庭で穏やかにふるまっていることで大成をするものなのだ．」

歴史家であるロビン・マンシーは，それにもかかわらず，女性参選論者はアメリカじゅうを草の根作戦で展開している，と述べている．

彼女たちは街から街へ，近隣の人たちを説得し，教会に来ている信者たちを説得し，また，州の代表議員に女性への参政権を与えるように説得しようとしているのである．

【Reading Comprehension Questions 解答】
1. F 2. F 3. T 4. T 5. F 6. F 7. T 8. F 9. F 10. T

【Listening Comprehension Questions 解答】
Hello, I'm Robyn Muncy. I'm a professor of (history) at the University of Maryland. Now, I'll mention the authority in the U.S. It is divided between the federal (government) and the states in the U.S. political system. That meant that women (who) wanted to have a right to vote in the late 19th century had a choice to join politics. In addition, (females) had much more authority at the state level. Around five out of one (hundred) females wanted to have a choice for election in the early 19th.

【English Composition 解答】
1. A new principal has been elected and is about to take office at the senior high school.
2. Many crowds agreed with the opposition of the majority opinion.
3. Women used to have been said that they were by nature nurturing, cooperative and thrived really within the confines of their own homes.

Unit 3. 自分で考えよう
【訳例】
こんにちは，ようこそ VOA Learning English の Words and Their Stories へ．

このプログラムでは，私たちがアメリカ英語でよく使われる慣用的な表現の使用法を説明している．また，それらの表現の起源も紐解いている．これらの慣用的に使われる表現の起源は一体どこから来ているのだろうか．

本日は，数字に関連する表現についての話題を取り上げたい．なぜかって．それは考えれば分かるはずだ．VOA では多くのプログラムを用意し，遅かれ早かれ，数字に関連する表現を習得できるようになっている．

「do the math」という動詞句は，特に，その答えがとてもはっきりしている場合に，ある結論に達するための正確な情報を分析することを意味している．

例えば，私が動物愛護者であると仮定しよう．私は野良猫や野良犬を世話することで，全ての貯金を費やす．私の友人は，私がなぜ休暇を取らないのか理由を尋ねると，私は飼っている7匹の猫と5匹の犬を単に指差し，「休暇のためのお金だって．状況を考えればわかるはずだ」というだろう．

もちろん，子供たちは実に，基本的な算数を学ぶ前に，数を数える方法を習得しなければなら

ない．

　しかしながら，数字を数えることは，「count」という単語を単に意味するわけではない．科学者であるアルベルト・アインシュタインによる有名な引用文を考えてみなさい．彼は「大事なものの全てが数えられるわけではない．数えられるもの全てが大事なわけではない」と繰り返し述べてきた．

　この引用文は，駄洒落，言葉遊び（語呂合わせ）である．その引用文は「count」という単語を2つの意味で解釈している．この単語は何かの総数を決定することを意味し，それはまた，価値観や重要性を持つことも意味している．考慮すべきことや重大なことなど，無視することはできない．

　ある会話の中で使われる「count」という単語を取り挙げよう．ある2人の友人が目前に迫ったアメリカ大統領選挙について話をしている．以下の会話の中で，「depend」を意味する「count」の第三の定義が使われていることに注目しなさい．

A：君は11月に選挙に行くの．
B：なぜ私が選挙に行かなければならないの．私の票は有効にはならない．
A：「票が有効にならない」ってどういうこと．投票所が閉まると，投票所の係員が全ての票を数えるよね．
A：私が言いたいのは，ワシントン・コロンビア特別区の有権者たちがアメリカ連邦議会において議員の議席を持っていないということだ．だから，大統領への私の票は，公式に集計されたとしても，私の近隣地域で起こりそうなことについての私の意見は考慮されない．そして，ワシントン・コロンビア特別区の多くの人々は，そのことにうんざりしている．君にもそのことがわかるだろ．
B：ああ，その通りだ．私はその事実を考慮していなかった．私はメリーランド州に住んでおり，アメリカ連邦議会に10人の議員がいる．だから私の声は，君の声以上に反映される．
A：なるほど．

　それは多くのことを考慮するということである．

　多くの子供たちは，数字を数えられるようになると，単純な足し算の問題を解くことを学ぶようになる．彼らは $1+1=2$ であることや，$2+2=4$ であることなどを学ぶのである．

【Reading Comprehension Questions 解答】
1. T　2. T　3. F　4. T　5. F　6. T　7. F　8. F　9. T　10. F

【Listening Comprehension Questions 解答】
Strong writing is one of the most（important）（skills）for any college student. Many non-native English speakers（have）（no）（idea）what professors in the U.S. expect from a college paper. A college paper is

a piece of writing than can be (as) (long) (as) 20 or more pages. Even native English-speaking college students (struggle) (with) how to succeed with such a difficult responsibility.

【English Composition 解答】
1. The math exam was not as difficult as I had expected.
2. I wish I had finished my homework last night.
3. Even if you have talent, you will probably fail if you don't work hard.

Unit 4. 2050年までに海洋には魚よりプラスチックが増えている
【訳例】
　今よりもっとリサイクルを行わないと，2050年までには世界の海にいる魚よりも多くのプラスチックが存在することになるだろう．そのことは世界経済協議会（WEF）と，エレン・マッカーサー財団が最新報告の中で警鐘を鳴らしている．
　その報告書では，もし現在の傾向が続けば，海は2025年には3トンの魚ごとに1トンのプラスチックを包含することになり，2050年までには，プラスチックは魚の総重量を越えるであろうと伝えている．
　問題は，毎年低く見積もっても800万トンのプラスチックが最終的に世界中の海へ流出することになるということである．
　報告書では，この懸念はゴミ収集車の中身を絶えず海の中へ放出することと同じことであると言及している．
　プラスチックボトルを水中へ投げ捨てる人がいるからといっても，全てのプラスチックが最終的に海へ流出して行くとは限らない．
　環境保護団体『マリーン・ディフェンス』によると，車道や歩道に投げ捨てられたプラスチック容器と他のごみ類は，頻繁に海の中へ流出して行き，それらの割れた破片が，暴風雨のときに排水管から運ばれるとの見解を示した．
　それらのごみ類の中には，最終的に渦の方へたどり着くものもある．渦はプラスチックを円の中に取り込んで動かす大きな渦巻きになる．
　海の中の他の種類のごみとは違って，プラスチックは決して生物分解をすることはない．それは，化学変化を起こさないということを意味する．
　海の中に流出するプラスチック量の流出を減速させる方法がある．つまり，人々はもっとリサイクルをしようと思えばできるのである．これは世界経済協議会（WEF）とエレン・マッカーサー財団による報告書の重要な勧告である．
　報告書の中で著者は，現在のところプラスチックの約14パーセントしかリサイクルされていないということと，ヨーロッパの調査では，利用可能な技術を用いて，プラスチックの53パーセントもの量がリサイクルされているということに言及している．

その報告書の中では，別の解決策として梱包している製品に対しプラスチックの使用を減らすことだと謳っているが，著者は，そのようなことは起こりそうにないという見解を示している．

プラスチック包装の多くの利点を考慮すると，使用されたプラスチック包装の量において，全体的に大幅な削減の見込みや望ましさの両方が明らかに低い水準になっているということが，その報告書の中で伝えられた．

しかし，著書はプラスチックの使用を減らすことが，可能なところで試されるべきであると指摘している．

数十年間，科学者はプラスチックによって魚が殺されていることに警鐘を鳴らしてきた．天然資源保護協議会は，魚がプラスチックを食べた後，窒息が原因で死に至るということを研究によって明らかになったということに言及し，その他の死因はプラスチックが『腸閉塞や飢餓』を引き起こすということを指摘した．

文責：マリオ・リッター

【Reading Comprehension Questions 解答】
1. F 2. T 3. T 4. F 5. T 6. T 7. F 8. T 9. F 10. F

【Listening Comprehension Questions 解答】
New efforts are underway to make American college campuses and public housing off limits to (cigarette) (smoking). Twenty colleges in the United States recently (received) (grants) to help make their campuses tobacco free. And in November, U.S. Housing and Urban Development Secretary Julian Castro announced that smoking will (become) (illegal) at all public housing over the next 18 months. (The) (federal) (housing) (department) has over one million homes.

【English Composition 解答】
1. Air pollution is a serious problem in many countries.
2. We must do what we can do to save energy.
3. Once you get into the habit of smoking, it is difficult to quit.

Unit 5. ジョージ・ワシントン：大統領，男，神話
【訳例】
　アメリカ人はジョージ・ワシントンのことを「私たちの国の父」と呼ぶ．

　ほとんどの人は彼が1789年から1797年までの間，アメリカの初代大統領であったことをよく知っている．だが，彼の功績は多岐にわたる．ワシントンは独立戦争において大陸軍を指揮した．彼はイギリスの支配から植民地を解放へ導いた．彼はまた，アメリカ合衆国憲法制定会議の議長でもあった．

私生活では，ワシントンは大きなウイスキー蒸留所と何千エーカーの土地を所有していた．彼は大きくて繁栄した農場を管理した．独立戦争が終結したとき，ワシントン将軍はヴァージニアのマウントバーノンと呼ばれる屋敷へ帰りたかった．

ジョゼフ・エリスは歴史家で，「閣下：ジョージ・ワシントン」という本を書いた．受賞歴を持つ作品の著者である．

「彼は大統領にはなりたがらなかった．アメリカ史上，ジョージ・ワシントンほど大統領になりたがらなかった大統領はいない．」

だが，他の有力者たちが彼に憲法下で初代大統領になるよう求めた．すべての選挙人が彼に投票した．ワシントンは責務としてその役割を引き受けた．

大統領としてのワシントン

ジョージ・ワシントンが1789年に大統領として宣誓したとき，本当の州連合という考えは，依然アイデアにしかすぎなかった．アメリカ人は社会的，経済的，民族的に繋がりを持たない集団だった．例えば，ペンシルベニア州の民族の四分の一はドイツ語しか話さない．新しい大統領は憲法下で社会的，政治的な連合体を作らなければいけないことになった．

だが，憲法には，大統領がそれをどうやって実現するか詳細に書かれていなかった．ダグ・ブラッドバーンは，マウントバーノンにあるワシントン図書館の創設者で，ジョージ・ワシントンは大統領の仕事を生み出したと言っている．

「政治家としての彼の力量を判断するときに人々が推量できないのは，どれほど国が未熟だったか，つまり存続する可能性がとても低かったということです．」

ワシントン大統領は，あとに続くすべての大統領に向けて多くの重要な先例を残した，とブラッドバーン氏は述べる．まず，彼は単なる名目上の長ではなく，決定権者なのであった．

彼は助言者による集団，つまり内閣を設立した．助言者たちは大統領の職務，すなわち行政部門のとても重要な役割を担った．ワシントンは省を導くための強い人々を選んだ．内閣の人々が強く反対する時もあったが，ワシントンは彼らを上手く統括した．

ワシントン大統領はまた，国家の公式通貨，外務省（今は国務省と呼ばれている）を創設した．彼は六人の判事で構成される最高裁判所も設立した．

さらに，ワシントンは，大統領は外交政策を策定するべきだとも言った．その権限は憲法では明確に記されていなかった．

ブラッドバーン氏は，ワシントンは自分の仕事をとても真摯に捉えていて，指針として憲法をいつも使っていたと言う．

「彼は単に公職を作って，それを正当化する方法を考えだそうとしていたのではなく，憲法と共に職務を全うしようとしていた．」

大統領として，ジョージ・ワシントンは国中を飛び回った．ロード・アイランドでは，トルーロにあるヘブライ人の集会にあてて手紙を書いた．その手紙はユダヤ人の権利について雄弁に書かれていた．ブラッドバーン氏はこの手紙を「非常に重要」だと言っている．ユダヤ人と彼らの宗教を支持することは当時，革命的な受容の行為であった．

【Reading Comprehension Questions 解答】
1. T 2. F 3. F 4. F 5. F 6. T 7. T 8. F 9. F 10. F

【Listening Comprehension Questions 解答】
Doug Bradburn says Washington was the right man to be the father of the country and first president. Mr. Bradburn, (like) many historians, calls George Washington the "(**indispensable**) (man)." He made ideas about American freedom and government real, and he showed that even the president would operate (under) (the) (rule) of law.

【English Composition 解答】
1. The new president would have to establish a social and political union under the Constitution.
2. Washington took his job very seriously and always used the Constitution as his guide.
3. Washington said the president should set foreign policy.

Unit 6. シカゴ・カブスがワールドシリーズを制覇
【訳例】
　「ワッツ・トレンディング・トゥディ」の時間です．
　シカゴ・カブスがワールドシリーズを制覇した．1908年以来初めてのワールドシリーズ制覇となった．
　木曜日，＃CubsWin のハッシュタグがアメリカ全土でトレンドとなった．
　100年以上，カブスは「愛すべき敗者」として知られてきた．チームはアメリカ全土に多くのファンがいるが，ビックゲームに勝つことはできないと思われてきた．
　そのすべてが木曜日の未明にオハイオ州クリーブランドで変わった．
　カブスは深夜過ぎにクリーブランド・インディアンズを8–7で破り，ワールドシリーズ制覇を決めた．カブスは劣勢の状況から制覇した．カブスは対戦成績1勝3敗から3連勝を果たし，ワールドシリーズ制覇した．
　ワールドシリーズは7番勝負で，7試合中4試合勝利したチームが優勝となる．
　この結果は多くのクリーブランドのファンを落胆させた．インディアンズの最後のワールドシリーズ制覇は1948年だ．
　カブスはこの年のベストチームの一つだった．しかし多くのファンは劣勢の状況から挽回できるとは思わなかった．
　ある専門家は，優勝する可能性は週はじめの時点でわずか15％しかなかったと語った．
　2016年はスポーツで予想外のチームが優勝をしたことが重なる年になりつつある．サッカーでは，レスター・シティが今年はじめにプレミア・リーグを制した時には，一部の人々がそのすごさをアメリカのファンに説明するのに，カブスがワールドシリーズを制覇することになぞらえ

た．言い換えれば，全く予想しえないことが起こったということだ．

　数か月後，カブスは勝った．

　アメリカ中の人びとがソーシャルメディアで勝利を祝っている．

　ツイッターで最も人気のある投稿の一つが，シカゴ・エリアにある小学校の入構記入用紙の写真だ．

　それは多くの親が，子供たちはカブスの試合を見るために夜遅くまで起きていたために学校に遅刻したと話したことを示している．

　多くの人々は，リグリー・フィールドの外に設置されたメッセージボードを映したビデオも気に入っている．ここはシカゴにあるカブスの本拠地である．

　試合が終わったとき，ボードが書き換えられ「カブス勝利！」，何千人もの人が祝いました．

　もう一つ，ツイッターでの人気投稿は，1993年に撮られた写真と予言です．その写真は，ある男性の高校の卒業アルバムで，写真の下に彼は「シカゴ・カブス，2016年のチャンピオン，君が最初に聞いた」と書いていた．

　多くの人々は予言を的中させた40歳過ぎの男性のことを信じられない．

　またあるシカゴの男性は，とても古いビールでカブスの優勝を乾杯した．彼がそのビールを冷蔵庫に入れたのは1984年だ．カブスが優勝するまで飲まないと約束したのだった．

　ついに，32年後に彼はビールを開け，飲むことができた．

　「ワッツ・トレンディング・トゥディ」ダン・フリーデルでした．

【Reading Comprehension Questions 解答】
1. T 2. T 3. F 4. F 5. T 6. F 7. T 8. F 9. T 10. T

【Listening Comprehension Questions 解答】
The year 2016 (is) (turning) (out) to be a year of unexpected winners in sports. When the Leicester City soccer team won England's championship earlier this year, some people explained (its) (significance) to American fans by (comparing) (it) (to) the Cubs winning the World Series. In other words, it was not expected to happen at all.

【English Composition 解答】
1. The Chicago Cubs won three games in a row to win the World Series.
2. The year 2016 is turning out to be a year of unexpected winners in sports.
3. He promised not to drink the beer until the Cubs won a championship

Unit 7. プログラムがアメリカの貧困家庭を救う

【訳例】

貧困から逃れたい家庭を助けるためのプログラムがアメリカのジョージア州で行われており，他州の見本となっている．

このプログラムは個人からの寄付とジョージア州都であるアトランタ市役所の共同計画である．

今日では，アトランタのイースト・レイク地区は住みやすい場所である．しかし20年前までは，治安が悪く，評判の悪い地区だった．

最近，VOA リポーターのクリス・シムキンスがイースト・レイクを訪れ，イースト・レイク財団会長のダニエル・ショイを取材した．この財団はこの地区の人々を助けるために設立された．

「20年以上前では，この地区はイースト・レイク・メドウズという開発プロジェクトの拠点でした．国内でもっとも治安の悪い集団住宅地でした．今では，もっとも将来性のある地区です．」

市と個人寄付による1.5億ドルが貧困家庭を援助するために費やされている．キャロル・ノートンは非営利の「パーパス・ビルト・コミュニティーズ」で働いている．地域のリーダーたちと協力してこの地区の改善を目指している．

「収入格差はたしかにこの問題の一つの要因だが，社会的流動性の欠如も大きな要因です．もしアメリカに住んでる人々が，仕事や収入，そして子どもに良い教育機会を与えるという正当な目標がないとしたら，私たちの民主主義の根幹が脅かされてしまいます．」

イースト・レイク・ヴィレッジには約2,100人が住んでいる．低所得層または中間所得層の人だけが入居を許可されている．集団住宅界限には銀行，食料品店のほかに，高額所得者の住む地区にあるような店もある．

イースト・レイクの若者たちには学業援助があるので，彼らは大学に通い，良い仕事に就くことが可能だ．

20年前は，この地域の平均的4人家族は4,500ドルを稼ぐのに苦労していた．ショイ曰く，現在の平均収入は20,000ドルである．

「昔はこの地区にたった14パーセントしか就業率がなかったのです．現在は協動している家族では100%の就業率です．劇的な家庭収入の増大を見てきたよ．」

ミッシェル・キャンベルと彼女の家族は2013年にイースト・レイクに来て以来，成功を身をもって体験してきた．キャンベルは集団住宅の運営を手伝っている．彼女は財産を蓄え，初めての家を購入する予定だ．

「このようなプログラムは，自助努力を促します．働くために移住する住居者はプログラムの対象であるためには，（週）30時間の労働を義務づけられます．目標は，このプログラムから離れることであり，家を探し，経済的に良い地位に移ることです．」

イースト・レイクの有力者たちが言うには，このプログラムの成功は貧困からの脱却のために何ができるのかを示した好例である．

【Reading Comprehension Questions 解答】
1. T 2. T 3. F 4. F 5. T 6. F 7. T 8. T 9. T 10. F

【Listening Comprehension Questions 解答】
The absolute idea of (income) (inequality) is part of the problem, but the lack of **social** (**mobility**) is just as big a problem. If people in America don't feel like they have a reasonable **shot** at working and (earning) (a) (better) (life) and creating a better opportunity for their children, I think our democracy (is) (threatened) at its very **core**.

【English Composition 解答】
1. A program designed to help families escape poverty in the American state of Georgia is serving as a model for other parts of the United States.
2. Twenty years ago, an average family of four in this neighborhood struggled to earn $4,500 a year.
3. The residents are required to work 30 hours or more in order to be on the program.

Unit 8. ロボットが支援できる農業
【訳例】
　アメリカのアイダホ州で，ロボットが果物の木と葡萄の蔓の間を移動している．農作業をしているのだ．
　「アイダボット」と呼ばれるこのロボットは試作品，つまりモデルである．アイダホ州ナンパにあるノースウェスト・ナザリーン大学のエンジニアチームがアイダボットを開発した．
　それは小さい戦車のように見えるが，搭載されているのは大砲ではなくカメラや無線周波数センサーである．アイダボットは果樹園の至るところをゆっくり動き，世話を必要とする木に化学薬品を吹きかける．
　アイダボットは，作物の見張りや収穫などの仕事もやる．

アイダボットの仕組み
　アイダボットは無線周波数識別センサーを使う．この処理には樹木やぶどうの蔓に取り付けられた電子機器を使って識別する．アイダボットが果樹園の至るところを移動しながら，植物に取り付けられている電子機器を読み取り，どんな世話をするべきなのかを知る．
　ジョッシュ・グリフィンはこのプロジェクトのリーダーの一人で，アイダボットの仕組みについて説明する．
　「アイダボットにプログラムを書いて，1番と5番の木が化学薬品を必要としているとします．それぞれの木には，無線周波数識別タグをもたせてあります．アイダボットはタグからの信号を頼りに，どの木がアイダボットのとなりにあるかを判断します．5番の木の隣にあるときは，アイダボットは5番に化学薬品を吹きかけますし，1番の隣にあるときは，アイダボットは1番の

樹に化学薬品を吹きかけます.」

　工学のグリフィン准教授は，アイダボットは単独で作業ができると言う．ドローン（小さい無人飛行機）のような他の技術とも協働で働くこともできる．

　ある実験で，ドローンに特殊カメラを搭載し，葡萄の蔓あるいは果物の木の画像を撮影した．この画像情報はコンピューター・プログラムによって処理される．画像の色がその農作物が必要とする化学薬品の量をロボットに知らせるのだ．

　グリフィンは，ロボットを使用することにより，農家は人件費を抑えられると言う．そのうえ，化学薬品の使用を減らすことも可能なので，環境にも優しい．

　「人間が手間をかけることなく，自動的に化学薬品を散布し，しかも低圧力なので，確実に届くべき所に届きます．他の場所にまで散布してしまうことはありません．」

フルーツ・カウンティンクグ・アプリケーション

　学生と教授で構成されるロボット・チームは，さらにアイダボットのためにフルーツ・カウンティング・アプリケーションを開発している．これは画像分析装置を使って，果物の収穫高を正確に見積もる．

　もう一人の工学准教授，デューク・ブラノンはこのプロジェクトでグリフィンと一緒に研究している．彼の説明では，このシステムは幾種類かのカメラ（カラー，近赤外線カメラ，ステレオカメラなど）を使う．アイダボットが果樹園の中を移動する際に，このカメラは一本一本の木を撮影する．

　「私たちはこの画像を使って，コンピューター・プログラムを作り，一本一本の果実の数を見積もるのです．」

　農家のマイケル・ウィリアムソンは，アイダホ州カルドウェルに果樹園を持っている．彼は，自分の農作物にこのコンピューター・プログラムを使ってみたいと言っている．

【Reading Comprehension Questions 解答】
1. T　2. F　3. T　4. T　5. T　6. F　7. T　8. T　9. F　10. T

【Listening Comprehension Questions 解答】
(How) (much) (would) (farmers) have to pay for this robot? Big pieces of farm equipment can be expensive. But Griffin estimates a basic IdaBot that uses (radio) (frequency) (identification) (technology) would be relatively low-cost.

【English Composition 解答】
1. It looks like a small military tank.
2. This process uses electronic devices on the trees or grapevines to identify them.
3. When it is next to tree five, it will spray chemicals on tree number five

Unit 9. 2016年大統領選は公民の教師にとって難題
【訳例】

　アメリカ大統領選挙運動を見るのは難しいことだっただろうか．

　中学生のクラスに説明しなければいけないと想像してみてもらいたい．

　4年ごとに，アメリカの教師たちは政府の役割を説明するのに，大統領選挙について生徒たちと話し合う．

　しかし今年は，社会科教師のなかには，選挙について話し合うのは困難だと報告している．候補者たちの振る舞いや政治討論に中身がないことを説明しなければいけないからである．

　ジャヴォーン・パーキンスはヴァージニア州アレクサンドリアのジョージ・ワシントン中学校で教えている．彼は生徒たちに（テレビ）選挙広告を見せて，説得のさせ方を考えさせることを好む．

　パーキンスが考えるには，12，13歳までが生徒たちにとって政府について考えはじめるのに良い年齢である．ところが，今年の選挙戦では，選挙運動の紆余曲折のために，それが難しくなっている．

　「かつてなら，私がただ話題を投げかけ，「ワシントンポスト」やCNN，ほかのウェブサイトを映し，先頭ページに行って，「さあ，話し合おう」と言うことができました．」

　パーキンスは，今年の場合，新聞の記事は8年生には必ずしも良い内容ではないと言う．その一例が，ドナルド・トランプ候補が，女性に対する性的侮辱発言をした暴露映像だ．

　トランプが身体障がい者をからかったとき，パーキンスはどうやってこのことを授業で話せばよいのか分からなかった．

　「このことが明るみに出たとき，私はこの話を切り出して話し合おうと思ったのですが，やめました．」

　パーキンスは生徒たちの関心を政治について教えることから，そらしてしまうと感じ，学校のいじめ防止努力のためにならないと感じた．

違いに気づく生徒たち

　生徒たちはこの問題に気がついているようだ．パーキンスが生徒たちに選挙運動が年々どのように変化していったかを質問したとき，生徒たちは政治状況が変わったことを感じていた．彼らは，現在は，以前と比べてより悪影響がある，もしくはひどいと言った．

　「昔の候補者たちはもっと礼儀正しく，筋が通っていた．彼らはおもに戦争などの重要課題に重点を置いていた．しかし今では，候補者はまるで，「なんでもいいから相手を攻撃してやろうぜ」みたいで，子供じみているし，ばかばかしい．この国に対する侮辱です．」

　パーキンスがいうには，選挙戦において重要課題に関する議論が欠如していることが，彼の仕事を難しくしている．

　「私としては，（政治的）課題を知ることができるような話題を選ぶことがますます少なくなっています．候補者に対してもです．本当の意味で」

【Reading Comprehension Questions 解答】

1. F 2. F 3. T 4. T 5. T 6. T 7. F 8. F 9. T 10. F

【Listening Comprehension Questions 解答】

While many teachers like to have **mock** debates in the classroom (before) (an) (election), even that exercise is risky. Brent Wathke, a teacher at DeLong Middle School, told *The New York Times* that (a) (debate) (could) (invite) students to say insulting words. Instead, he had his class talk about the election campaign using "Socratic circles." He (separated) (the) (students) (into) small groups, and had them use work sheets to answer questions that he asked.

【English Composition 解答】

1. Every four years, teachers in the United States explain how the government works by talking with students about the presidential campaign.
2. He likes to have students watch campaign advertisements to look for their tools of persuasion.
3. When Trump made fun of a disabled person, Perkins was again not sure how to talk about it with his class.

Unit 10. バターを抜くこと！ 休暇の伝統に合わせた現代の食事

【訳例】

アメリカでは，年末の休暇に人々が贅沢で大量の食事をするのが主要行事となっている．

アメリカの人々は11月の第3木曜日に感謝祭を祝う．世界中の人々は12月25日にクリスマスを祝う．

どちらの休暇もごちそうを作る伝統がある．この休暇中の食事の食材には，通常大量の砂糖，塩，バターが使われる．この休暇中の最も一般的な食材は七面鳥とパイだ．

テリプライスは毎年クリスマス前の土曜日に開催するホリデーパーティーを30年間主催してきた．

「私の子ども達が幼い時に始めました．実は当初は一回しか実施しませんでした．パーティーは自分に贈るクリスマスプレゼントのようなものです．30年間の大半は多くのごちそうの準備に費やしてきました．」

しかし時が経つにつれていくつかの伝統は変わる．ネベルダイン一家は自分たちが食べる物を変えることでもっと健康になろうと思っている．ネベルダイン家の第一子であるミック・フリーは，この変化は休暇中や一年を通じた他の日も重要だと述べている．

「休暇は，実際には最も刺激的な時間とも言えます．なぜなら，有機栽培を使った健康的で楽しい方法で伝統料理を食べることができるかどうかを見極める機会だからです．そして私たちはそれを他人には言いません．『ここにトルコのごちそうがあるぞ』とはいいません．でもそのうち，

人々がトルコ料理を好きだと分かったら，私たちは『トルコ料理は自然食品だよ．すばらしいよ』というでしょう．」

ミックと恋人のミシェルは，自然食品だけを食べる努力をしている．自然食品は，不自然な化学物質の添加や加工を行わずに作られた植物性または動物性食品だ．

アメリカ農務省（USDA）は，食品に関する法律を制定するアメリカ政府の一機関である．USDA は，2002 年からどの食品が自然食品かの特定を開始した．

ミックは，恋人がグルテンを食べると気分が悪くなったと気づくと，自然食品だけを食べることにした．グルテンは小麦を含む食品に含まれている．ミックは自分が買った食品の成分をさらに詳しく調べ始めた．ほとんどの食品に含まれている不自然な成分の量に彼は驚いた．

しかし，ネベルディン家で食事を変えたのはミックだけではない．ミックの妹であるフェリシア・ネベルディンは，9 年前に完全菜食主義者になることを決意した．完全菜食主義者とは，どんな動物性食品も食べたり使用したりしない人間である．

フェリシアは，動物の扱いと動物農場の環境への影響を懸念して完全菜食主義者になった．彼女は食事を変えることで自分の健康状態が改善されたと語った．

「私は胃や消化力に多くの問題を抱えていましたが，完全菜食主義者になってからは，毎日より良い状態になっていると感じます．」

この特別な食事をするという選択は，ネベルディン家が慎重に食べ物を選ぶことを意味する．ミックは自宅の裏にある庭で新鮮な野菜を育てている．ネベルディン家はまた，牛乳やバターのないマッシュポテトのような伝統的な休日の食べ物を作る．

【Reading Comprehension Questions 解答】
1. T 2. F 3. T 4. F 5. T 6. T 7. F 8. F 9. F 10. T

【Listening Comprehension Questions 解答】
Studies (show) that high (calorie) diets can (cause) people to (become) overweight. The Centers for Disease Control, or CDC, is the top national (public) (health) organization in the U.S. A 2014 report from the CDC (showed) (69) percent of adults in the U.S. over (20) years old are (overweight).

【English Composition 解答】
1. People in the US celebrate Thanksgiving on the third Thursday of November.
2. Mick began looking more closely at the ingredients in the food he bought.
3. Felicia became a vegan because of her concern for the treatment of animals and the environmental effects of animal farming.

Unit 11. アメリカの郡の 3 分の 1 が出生率よりも死亡率のほうが高い

【訳例】

　最近，VOA はアメリカにおける郡の重要性について報告した．

　現在，米国国勢調査局が「州政府の主要な政治および行政部門」と呼ぶ郡にはさらに多くの事柄がある．

　全国には 3,000 を超える郡がある．

　大部分の州は，これらの下位区分を説明したり，より大きな領域内の区域を分けたりするために「郡」という用語を使用している．もちろん，この定義には例外がある．例えば，ルイジアナ州の南部は教区に分かれている．

　国勢調査局は，2010 年から 2015 年の間に 1,653 の郡が，人口が減ったと報告している．これは全国の郡全数の半分を超える．同時に，一般人口は約 4% 増加した．

　デラウェア州とハワイ州の 2 州だけが，人口減少の郡が全くない州である．

　新たな移住者を考慮しなければ，アメリカの 194 を超える郡の人口が減少している．

　全数の 3 分の 1 を超える郡で死亡者数が出生者数を上回っている．人口専門家はこれを「自然減少」と呼んでいる．しかし，それは必ずしも人口が減少しているとは限らない．

　郡の人口は，出生者数よりも死亡者数が多い場合でも増加することがある．その理由とは何か．人々はアメリカの他の地域や他国から移住して来るのだ．

　出生数より死亡者数が多い「瀕死の郡」と記載しているニュースもいくつかある．2009 年に，国勢調査局は 880 郡の人口が自然減少したと報告した．2012 年，国勢調査局は 1,135 の郡が自然減少したと概算した．そのほとんどが農村部である．

　ケネス・ジョンソン氏は，ニューハンプシャー大学の社会学教授である．同教授は AP 通信に対し，自然減少を伴う郡の数は，これらの地域の死亡者よりも出生が少ないという理由だけではなく，増加していると語った．同氏は，「ベビーブーマー」世代の死亡者数増加がもう一つの理由だと述べた．ベビーブーマーという用語は，1946 年から 1964 年の間に出生したアメリカ人 7,000 万人を表すために使われている．

　ジョンソン教授は，「将来的に自然減が続くと予想しています．これらの郡は急降下するスパイラル状態です．若者たちは去り，高齢者はそこに留まり年を取っていくのです．」

　同教授はさらに続ける．「若いヒスパニック系の人々を誘致するための，食肉化工場などの新たな開発といった大きな変化がなければ，これらの地域はさらに自然減少する可能性が高いです．」

　農村部の約 46% が自然減少を経ている．これは人口密集地域となった郡の 17% に相当する．

　専門家によると，それらの農村部の郡は，住民がますます高齢化し，出生率が低くなり，経済的に貧弱となるため「死ぬ」ことになる．専門家らは，地域によっては若者達を維持し，惹きつけることは難しいと言っている．

　日本と多くのヨーロッパ諸国は，長年自然減少を経験している．

　アメリカでは，カリフォルニア州，アリゾナ州，ネバダ州などの 10 大郡が西部にある．最小

郡のいくつかは東部の州に所在している．

【Reading Comprehension Questions 解答】
1. T 2. T 3. F 4. F 5. T 6. F 7. T 8. F 9. F 10. T

【Listening Comprehension Questions 解答】
Five of the (10) smallest (counties) by (population) (are) in the state of Nebraska. Cook County, Illinois, which (includes) Chicago, is the second-most-populous county in the nation. It (has) more (people) than 29 (states) and more than the seven (smallest) (states) combined.

【English Composition 解答】
1. Meg Grigal works with an organization called Think College.
2. There is a campaign to encourage young people with mental disabilities to consider college.
3. VCU discovered one student who had no idea how artistic he was.

Unit 12. 侮辱的な地名は変えるべきか
【訳例】
　アメリカの何百もの場所が，スコー・クリーク，スコー・フラット，スコー・メドウズ，スコー・スプリングスなど「スコー」という単語を使用している．1960年，冬季オリンピックがカリフォルニア州にあるスコーバレーというスキー場で開催された．
　しかし，その言葉が不快と感じる人もいる．これは，アメリカ先住民の女性または妻に関する古い言い方だ．多くの辞書は，その言葉が侮辱的とみなされていると記載している．もう会話でその言葉を使う人はほとんどいない．
　現在，議員やボランティアの中には，「スコー」という単語や他の侮辱的な単語を含む土地の名称を変更しようとする人々もいる．
　人種や民族に対する侮辱の歴史
　スコー・バレーのような地名は歴史的だが，人種や民族に対する侮辱がアメリカ社会の共通部分だった時代の名残でもある．
　人種や民族のあだ名を含む他の土地に「ネグロ・ベン・マウンテン」「ユダ・バレー」「チャイナマンズハット」「レッドマン・クリーク」などがある．
　VOAは一般的にニュースの一部でない限り，これらの名前や他のより攻撃的な名前を放送することはなく，ウェブサイトにその名称を掲載しない．しかし，多くの人々がこれらの名称を使い続けている．そしてその名称をいまだに地図や看板に表示していることが多い．
　6州の議員らは，州で論争の的になっている地名の変更を強制するか，提案する法案をすでに承認している．委員会は，たとえその名称によって侮辱される人々がいても歴史的な名前を残す

ことが許容できるか否かを決定しなければならない．

30を超える侮辱的な名称

米国北西部のワシントン州は，その地名を慎重に検討している土地の1つである．

プラミラ・ジャイパルはワシントン州の上院議員だ．同氏は，侮辱的な名称となっている地名のリストを作成するように天然資源省のワシントン州支局を説得した．その後，同氏はその支局報告書を公表した．

天然資源省当局は36の名称を見つけている．その中には「ジム・クロウ・ポイント」「ジム・クロウ・クリーク」などが含まれている．

アメリカ英語では，「ジム・クロウ」という名前はもともと黒人に対する侮辱的な用語だった．この用語は，南北戦争後の1870年代から人種差別を禁止する連邦政府の公民権法が議会で可決された1950年代，1960年代までアメリカで施行された人種隔離を強制した法律を示すために使用されたものだった．

「ジム・クロウ・ポイント」と「ジム・クロウ・クリーク」は，19世紀に海軍から脱走し，その土地に住み着いた黒人の名前から命名されたと信じている人々もいる．

しかし，一部の地域住民は異なる信念を持っている．ある情報筋によると，この名称は地元の川近くにある木々に生息するクロウ（カラス）という鳥の名前に由来している．

また，もう一人近くに住むジョー・バドニック氏によると，ジム・クロウ・ポイントとジム・クロウ・クリークは先住民の首長にちなんで名づけられたという．

バドニック氏は引退した漁師であり，トラック運転手でもあった．同氏は，地元の人々が州政府職員が地元の地名を変更すると述べているのを好まないと語っている．

「彼らは私たちが人種差別主義者であり，愚かであり，そうではない場合も，他人や他の全ての事柄に攻撃していることを知らなかったというのです」と苦言を呈している．

政治的圧力に対してバドニック氏は反対していたが，いくつかの代替名を提案した．同氏は，その地域にブルックフィールドと呼ばれた町が存在していたため，ジム・クロウ・ポイントはブルックフィールド・ポイントと命名することもできると述べている．

そして同氏は，昔その地域に定住した家族を称えるために，ジム・クロウ・クリークはハーローズ・クリークに，ジム・クロウ・ヒルはベア・ヒルと命名することができるとも言っている．名称の提案を検討する州委員会は，バドニック氏のアイデアに好意的だった．委員会委員は最終審査の際，その名称を承認した．

【Reading Comprehension Questions 解答】
1. T　2. F　3. T　4. T　5. F　6. F　7. T　8. T　9. F　10. F

【Listening Comprehension Questions 解答】
Jon Shannon（lives）on one of the（islands）. He（says）he would never（call）someone a "squaw."

But, he (says), "there is a difference between (making) it personal and the history that (goes) along with the place names that (have) (been) (assigned) historically. I (guess) I just don't see anything wrong with that."

【English Composition 解答】
1. Place names such as Squaw Valley are historic, but they are also signs of a time when racial and ethnic insults were a common part of American society..
2. Committees must decide whether to keep a historical name even if some people may be insulted by it.
3. Committee members approved them for final consideration.

Unit 13. 4組に1組のアメリカ人夫婦は夫と妻が同じ宗教を共有していない

【訳例】
　アメリカの結婚した成人の25%は，夫または妻とは異なる宗教的信仰を持っている．
　それはキリスト教徒の母親とユダヤ教徒の父親，または非常に宗教的な母親とそうではない父親かもしれない．
　この情報は，ワシントンDCの独立した研究グループであるピュー・リサーチ・センターの情報である．このセンターは，2014年に3万5,000人のアメリカ人に対して行った意見調査の調査結果に基づいて発表を行った．

　母親が一番よく知っている
　ピュー・センターによると，異なる宗教的信仰を持つ両親の家庭で育った子ども達は，母親の影響を最も受けることが判明した．
　同センターの報告によると，母親の宗教を信仰する混合宗教家庭で育った人は48%だった．父親の宗教を信仰する家庭は28%に過ぎない．
　混合宗教の家庭で育ったおよそ4人に1人は両親の宗教的信仰のいずれも信仰していない．

　宗教的信仰の共有はどれほど重要か
　ピュー・センターが調査した人々は，同じ宗教的信仰を配偶者と共有することが彼らにとってどれほど重要かについて質問を受けた．
　回答者の44%が成功する結婚には同じ宗教的信仰を共有することが非常に重要だと述べた．しかし，その数字は他の理由が重要だとするアメリカ人の割合と比較して高いとは言えないとピュー・センターは述べている．
　60%を超える高い割合で，回答者は，成功する結婚には興味の共有，満足のいく性的関係，家事の分担が非常に重要であると考えている．
　回答者が成功する結婚には十分なお金を持っていることが非常に重要だと答えた割合は46%

だった．その割合は，宗教的信仰の共有が非常に重要であると回答した割合よりも高かった．

同じ宗教を持つ人と結婚した人々の62％が，結婚を決定するのに非常またはある程度重要であると答えている．

宗教を特定していない人々の84％が結婚の決定において配偶者の宗教的信仰は重要ではないと述べている．

同センターは，同じ宗教的信仰を共有していない家庭で育ったアメリカ人の数は増えていると発表している．

同センターの報告によると，2010年以降に結婚した人々の39％が異なる宗教的信仰を持つ配偶者がいる．

1960年以前に結婚した夫婦で異なる宗教の人と結婚したのは19％にすぎないと同センターは述べている．

ピュー・センターによると，アメリカ人の宗教的構成も変化している．

キリスト教は依然としてアメリカの主要な宗教である．ピュー・センターの調査対象の人々の70％以上は，2014年には自分をキリスト教徒と表現していた．その割合は2007年の78.4％から下がっている．

アメリカ人の約1.9％が自分はユダヤ人であると述べており，2007年の1.7％から増加している．イスラム教徒は人口の0.9％を占めており，2007年の0.4％から増加している．

2014年には，アメリカ人の22.8％がどの宗教も信仰していないと述べており，この数値は2007年の16.1％から増加している．組織化されている宗教を信じない人々や神の教えを信じるが，一つの宗教を信仰していない人々もいる可能性がある．

【Reading Comprehension Questions 解答】
1. T 2. F 3. F 4. T 5. T 6. F 7. T 8. F 9. T 10. F

【Listening Comprehension Questions 解答】
(Twenty-five) (percent) of married adults in the United States (have) different religious beliefs than their husband or wife.

That (could) (be) a Christian mother and a Jewish father, or a very religious mother and a father who is not (religious).

This information (comes) (from) the Pew Research Center, an (independent) research group in Washington, D.C. The center (based) its findings on a 2014 opinion survey of 35,000 Americans.

【English Composition 解答】
1. Children raised in homes with parents of different religious beliefs were most influenced by their mothers.
2. Forty-four percent said sharing the same religious beliefs is very important to a successful marriage.

3. Christianity is still the major religion in the United States.

Unit 14. ビービー・ワイナンズ音楽，神そして家族
【訳例】
　シンガーソングライターのビービー・ワイナンズの歌声だ．彼の出生時の名前はベンジャミンだが，現在皆には「ビービー」という名前で知られている．
　ビービーはキリスト教徒の大家族出身だ．彼の両親デロレスとデビッド・ワイナンズは，7人の息子と3人の娘を育てた．
　ワイナンズは，音楽，神と家族は自分を養育してくれた基盤だと述べている．
　「私は家族の中で成長し，音楽を中心に育ち，神をあがめ，取り巻く家族の中で成長しました．私たちが教会に行くと，そこは家族であり，私の基盤だったと思っています．それは私が家を出てミシガン州デトロイトを離れて以来ずっと抱えてきた気持ちです．
　17歳のビービーとシーシーと呼ばれる15歳の妹プリシラはノースカロライナ州パインビルに向かうため家を出た．彼らは，人気のあるキリスト教テレビ番組「PTLクラブ」でバックコーラスの歌手としてプロのキャリアを歩み始めた．PTLは神である主を賛美する番組だった．
　ワイナンズは，ショーの主催者であるジム・ベイカーとタミー・フェイ・ベイカーは，彼と妹を家族として扱ったと語っている．番組に出演している間に兄妹は最初のアルバム「神が我らを高めてくださる」をPTLレコードとして録音した．
　1987年に，ワイナンズは「PTLクラブ」を去った．同年，彼らは最初のアルバム「ビービー＆シーシー・ワイナンズ」をリリースした．主流のアルバムは，「アイ・オー・ユー・ミー」という曲が彼らにとって最初のリズム・アンド・ブルースのヒット曲となった
　兄と妹は5枚のアルバムをともに録音した．1995年に，彼らはソロとしてのキャリアを究めることにした．
　ビービー・ワイナンズは作詞家として，いつも，ゴスペルやコンテンポラリーのどの歌でも自分の精神性を表現できると分かっていたと言う．
　「私が他の人と作詞する中で際立たせたものは，私の関係性，家族，仕事，あらゆるもの，演劇，人生の全視点などであり…人生のあらゆる領域で神が何を意味しているのかを話すことができると感じていたのです．だから私は人生でゴスペルのカテゴリーに入らない歌に感動しました．ですから，ご存じの「家路につく」「愛してはいない」「君無しではいられない」「合間に」などの曲は全て私の人生を反映しているのです．」
　ビービー・ワイナンズは複数のソロアルバムをリリースし，6回グラミー賞受賞経験がある．同氏はまた，他の歌手にヒットソングを作詞，作曲している．また俳優や作家でもある．
　同氏の最新の仕事は自分の人生に関するミュージカルだ．ワイナンズと家族の友人でディレクターでもあるチャールズ・ランドルフ・ライトは「このために生まれた．ビービー・ワイナンズ物語」をともに著した．

アーティストであるビービーは，シンガーソングライターのロバータ・フラックとの電話の会話から始まったと言っている.

「ミュージカルは電話から始まりました．それはロバータ・フラックとの電話でした．そして，私たちはミュージカル以外のこと全てについて話していました．会話の途中から，彼女は遠まわしに言ったのです．『ビービー，いつあなたとあなたの家族についてのミュージカルを書くつもりなの』ってね．アメリカ人のミュージカルです．物語だったのです．その後映画になるとのことでした．電話から４日後，私はモントリオールのホテルにいました．私は歩き，ノートパソコンを開け，蛇口をひねるようなものでした．そしてその場で，現在「このために生まれてきた」の最初の草稿を書いたのです．」

【Reading Comprehension Questions 解答】
1．T 2．F 3．F 4．T 5．F 6．T 7．F 8．T 9．T 10．F

【Listening Comprehension Questions 解答】
It (talks) (about) coming of age of two young (African) (Americans) being thrust from a (childhood) up until that point of predominantly a (black) situation and then thrust into a world that was predominantly a white situation. So we endured racism, we endured a lot of things, but just a (culture) (shock), you know. (Different) worlds, you know. It talks about (finding) myself.

【English Composition 解答】
1. Winans says music, God and family were the foundation of his upbringing.
2. The brother and sister recorded five albums together.
3. BeBe Winans has several solo albums and six Grammy awards.

ミニ TOEIC テスト解答編

Test 1　テスト 1（問題数 17 題）

Listening test

Part 1

　Directions: For each question, you will hear four statements about a photo in your test book. After listening to the statements, please select the one that best describes what you see in the photo.
1. Look at picture number 1 in your test book.

【訳】
リスニングテスト
パート 1
　指示：写真について４つの説明が聞こえます．その説明を聞き，写真を最もよく記述している

アルファベット選択しなさい．

写真 1 を見なさい．

(A) People are waiting in line for their turn.

(B) She is standing in the aisle of the store.

(C) The price tag is being replaced.

(D) The plants are being watered.

【解答】(B)

【解説】女性が店の通路に立っている写真である．

【訳】

(A) 人々は自分の番を待っている．

(B) 彼女は店の通路に立っている．

(C) 価格札を置き換えている．

(D) 植物に水をやっている．

Part 2

Directions: You will hear a statement or question and three answers in English. They are printed on your test book and will be played once. Please select the best answer to the statement or question.

【訳】

パート 2

指示：説明または質問とそれに対する回答例が 3 件英語で一度だけ話されます．回答として最も適切なものを選択しなさい．

2. Which sweater do you want?

(A) I would like more.

(B) **The red one.**

(C) A twenty percent discount.

【解答】(B)

【訳】

2. あなたはどんなセーターがほしいですか．

  (A) 私はもっと欲しいです．

  (B) 赤いほうです．

  (C) 20％割引です．

3. Where can I ride a train to New York?

  (A) Yes, I rode it.

  (B) **At the east terminal.**

  (C) A fifteen-minute walk.

【解答】(B)

【訳】

3. どこでニューヨーク行の電車に乗れますか．

  (A) はい．私はそれに乗りました．

  (B) イーストターミナルです．

  (C) 歩いて15分です．

Part 3

Directions: You will hear conversations between two or more people. You will be asked three questions about what the speakers discuss in each conversation. Please select the best answer to each question. The conversations are not printed in your test sheet and are played once.

Questions 4 through 6 are related to the following conversation:

【訳】

パート3

指示：複数の人による会話が聞こえます．話題について3つ質問されます．各質問に最も適した答えを選択してください．会話はテスト用紙には印刷されず，一度だけ再生されます．

次の会話に関連する4～6の質問に答えなさい．

A: Hello, I'd like to purchase a ticket for the ten o'clock bus to Atlanta.

B: Unfortunately, ma'am, that bus is already full.

A: Oh, really? Well, what should I do?

C: Here's a copy of the daily bus schedule, ma'am. Why don't you look it over and choose a later departure? At this time, buses to Atlanta leave frequently.

A: Hmmm … if I wait for the 12:40 bus, I'll have time to buy souvenirs for my family before leaving. Do you know if there's a shop in the bus terminal?

B: Yes, there's one down the stairs and to the right.

A: O.K. Thank you very much.

C: My pleasure, have a nice day, ma'am.

【訳例】

A：こんにちは，アトランタ行きの10時のバスのチケットを購入したいのですが．

B：お客様，残念ながら，そのバスはすでに満員です．

A：ああ，本当ですか．さて，どうしたらいいかしら．

C：お客様，毎日のバス時刻表コピーです．お客様，今後の出発便を選んでみたらいかがですか．この時間帯は，アトランタ行きのバスは頻繁に出発しています．

A：そうねえ，12時40分のバスを待つと，出発するまでに家族のお土産を買う時間がありますね．バスターミナルにはお店がありますか．

B：はい，階段を下って右にあります．

A：わかりました．ありがとうございます．

C：どういたしまして．素敵な一日をお過ごしください．

4. Where is the conversation taking place?

   (A) **At a bus terminal.**
   (B) At a car rental agency.
   (C) At a train station.
   (D) At an airport.

【解答】（A）

【解説】アトランタ行のバスのことを聞いているので，バスターミナルであると分かる．

【訳】

4. 会話はどこで行われていますか．

   (A) バスターミナル
   (B) レンタカー代理店
   (C) 駅
   (D) 空港

5. What does staff C suggests the questioner do?

   (A) Talk in the lobby.
   (B) Call a taxi agent.
   (C) **Look at a bus schedule.**
   (D) Drop her baggage.

【解答】(C)

【解説】C はバスの時刻表を見て，今後出発するバスにしてはどうかと勧めている．

【訳】

5. スタッフ C は質問者に何を提案していますか．

    (A) ロビーで話すこと

    (B) タクシー会社に電話すること

    (C) バスの時刻表を見ること

    (D) 彼女の荷物を預けること

6. Where will the questioner probably go next?

    (A) To a ticket machine.

    (B) To a department store.

    (C) To a telephone booth.

    (D) **To a souvenir shop.**

【解答】(D)

【解説】家族にお土産を買う時間がありそうだと話し，店はあるかと聞いているので，土産物店に行くと考えられる．

【訳】

6. 次に質問者はどこに行きますか．

    (A) 改札機

    (B) 百貨店

    (C) 電話ボックス

    (D) 土産物店

Part 4

Directions: You will listen to a single person speaking. You will be asked three questions about what the speaker says. Please select the best answer to each question. The dialogue is not printed in your test sheet and will only be played once.

Questions 7 through 9 concern the following text:

【訳】

パート 4

指示：一人が話します．その内容について 3 つ質問が出されます．各質問に対する最も適切な回答を選択してください．話の内容はテスト用紙には印刷されず，一度だけしか再生されません．

次の文章に関する質問 7 ～ 9 に答えなさい．

Yesterday evening, the governor announced that the province will begin construction on a new arts center. The building will be named after George Johnson, an influential music teacher who has worked in the Brookings Building School for over 40 years. The arts center will accommodate various groups of artists. Construction will continue through the spring and summer months. In November, local singers, actors and dancers will put on a free show on the main stage to celebrate the center's opening. All community members in this province are welcome to join.

【訳例】

昨夕，知事は州が新たに芸術センターの建設に着手すると発表した．この建物は，ブルッキングス・ビルディング・スクールで40年以上働いている著名な音楽教師であるジョージ・ジョンソンにちなんで命名されます．芸術センターは，様々なアーティストグループの催しを行います．センター建設は春から夏にかけて行われます．11月には地元の歌手，俳優，ダンサーがセンターの開設を祝うためにメインステージで無料のショーを行う予定です．州の全地域住民の方々の参加を歓迎します．

7. What is the announcement mainly about?

  (A) A new store.

  (B) A music school project.

  (C) A new arts center.

  (D) Local community members.

【解答】(C)

【解説】新たに芸術センターを建設すると知事が述べたとある．(C)が正解．

【訳】

7. 発表は主に何を述べていますか．

  (A) 新店舗

  (B) 音楽学校プロジェクト

  (C) 新しい芸術センター

  (D) 地域社会のメンバー

8. Who is George Johnson?

  (A) A singer.

  (B) A governor.

  (C) An architect.

  (D) A teacher.

【解答】(D)

【解説】ジョージ・ジョンソンは著名な音楽教師である．

【訳】

8. ジョージ・ジョンソンはどんな人ですか．

（A）歌手

（B）知事

（C）建築家

（D）教師

9. According to the speaker, what will happen in November?

（A）A policy will go into effect.

（B）Tickets will go on sale.

（C）**A show will be performed.**

（D）A lecture will start.

【解答】（C）

【解説】話者によると，11月には開設を祝うショーが行われる．

【訳】

9. 話者による，11月には何がありますか．

（A）政策が施行される

（B）チケットが発売される

（C）ショーが行われる

（D）講義が始まる

Reading Test

リーディングテスト

You will read various texts and answer related questions.

テスト問題を読んで質問に答えなさい．

Part 5

Directions: A word or phrase is missing in each sentence. Select the best answer to complete the sentence.

【訳】

パート5

指示：各文で抜けている単語または語句の答えを選択し，文を完成させなさい．

10. Factory tests **have** helped Asix Company to improve the design of its popular dress.

【訳】

工場で行われた試験により，Asix社は，人気の高い服のデザインの改善に役立てました．

(A) has

(B) **have**

(C) has been

(D) had being

【解答】(B)

【解説】主語が tests なので複数形であり，そこからの時制，かつ「試験が支援をした」ので，能動態で記されることにより (B) have が入る．

11. Any mechanical malfunction equipment should **be** reported to the manager immediately.

【訳】

器具に不具合が生じた時には，どのような場合であれ責任者に即座に報告をしてください．

(A) **be**

(B) been

(C) being

(D) have

【解答】(A)

【解説】主語が Any mechanical malfunction equipment とものになっていることから受け身である事がわかる．したがって「助動詞 + be + 過去分詞」になるので，(A) be が入る．

Part 6

Directions: Read the following texts. A sentence, phrase or word is missing in each text. Select the best answer to complete the sentence.

Questions 12-13 refer to the following notice.

【訳】

パート 6

指示：次の文章を読んでください．問題文の文，フレーズ，単語が抜けている箇所があります．最も適切な答えを選択し，文章を完成させてください．

以下の質問 12 と 13 に答えなさい．

Training for Sales Staff

Delaware Publishing is committed to the success and productivity of its entire sales staff, and we would like to hear 12. **from** you. The training office at Delaware Publishing has put together a schedule of workshops on computer skills and sales techniques for the next year. We invite your suggestions for topics that you imagine would 13. **benefit** you in the performance of your current job responsibilities.

【訳】

販売社員の研修

デラウェア出版では，全販売社員の成功と生産性向上に努めておりますので，社員みなさんからのご意見をお聞きしたいと存じます．デラウェア出版の研修課では次年度に際して，コンピューターの操作技術や営業技術についての研修会の予定をしています．現在の業務を行っていく上で有用であると思われる題材について，ぜひご提案ください．

12.
  (A) on
  (B) **from**
  (C) at
  (D) in

【解答】(B)

【解説】文意より「～から連絡が来る」という意味になるので，(B) from「～から」が入る．

【訳】
  (A) ～の上に
  (B) ～から
  (C) ～で
  (D) ～の中に

13.
  (A) suggest
  (B) advantage
  (C) **benefit**
  (D) react

【解答】(C)

【解説】文意より「現在の業務を行っていく上で有用であると思われる題材について」となることから，(C) benefit「有益である」が入る．

【訳】
  (A) 提案する
  (B) 有利である
  (C) 有益である
  (D) 反応する

Part 7

Directions: You will read a selection of texts, including e-mails, magazine and newspaper articles, and advertisement messages. Several questions follow the texts. Please select the best answer.

Questions 14 and 15 refer to the following texts.

【訳】

パート7

指示:電子メール,雑誌や新聞記事,広告メッセージなどから出題する文章です.その文章に対する複数の質問の最も適切な答えを選択してください.

以下の14～15の質問に答えなさい.

Fabric Manufacturers Exhibition

Blue River Hotel, 65 Cherry Street, Goldtown, NC 27211

Event Schedule: Friday, March 25

Keynote Talk by Nancy Smith, 8:30-9:30 a.m., Main Exhibition Room

The president of the Fabric Manufacturers Association will welcome attendees to the conference.

Fashion Trend Prediction of Designers by Anne Holding, 9:30-10:30 a.m., Stefan Room

The speaker will discuss upcoming trends in fabrics for casual women's clothing.

New Ways in Clothing Design by Peter Keller, 10:30-11:30 a.m., Samuel Room

The speaker will examine how designers use fabric to create shape and movement in their clothes.

Displays, 1:00-5:30 p.m., Exhibitors Hall

Over 40 fabric manufacturers will exhibit samples of their latest fabrics.

Fashion Show conducted by Nancy Smith, 5:30-8:00 p.m., Hotel Atrium

Please enjoy the collection of five active fashion designers using the most popular fabrics.

【訳例】

繊維メーカーの展示会

〒27211 ノースカロライナ州,ゴールドタウン,チェリーストリート65,ブルーリバーホテル

イベント開催日:3月25日(金)

開催の辞 ナンシー・スミス,午前8時30分～9時30分,メイン展示室

繊維メーカー協会会長が会議参加者の皆様に歓迎の挨拶を致します.

デザイナーのためのファッショントレンドの展望 — アン・ホールディング,午前9時30分～10時30分,ステファンルーム

カジュアルな婦人服地に関する今後のトレンドについて,講演者がお話しします.

服飾デザインの新しい手法 — ピーター・ケラー,午前10時30分～11時30分,サミュエルルーム デザイナーがどう布地を使い服の形を完成させ,動的効果を生み出すかを講演者が分析し

ます．

　　展示 — 午後1時〜5時30分，展示ホール
　　40社を超える繊維メーカーが最新の布地サンプルを展示します．
　　ファッションショー．司会進行ナンシー・スミス，午後5時30分〜8時，ホテルアトリウム
　　5名の売れっ子ファッションデザイナーが最近最も流行している布地の使い方をご覧に入れます．

14. Who is Ms. Smith?
　　(A) **An association president.**
　　(B) An emerging fashion designer.
　　(C) A clothing store owner.
　　(D) A hotel manager.

【解答】(A)

【解説】本文4行目にNancy Smith の所属と役職名「The president of the Fabric Manufacturers Association will welcome attendees to the conference.」があることからわかる．

【訳】
14. スミスさんとは誰ですか．
　　(A) 協会会長
　　(B) 新鋭のファッションデザイナー
　　(C) 服飾店経営者
　　(D) ホテルマネージャー

15. Where will the fashion show take place?
　　(A) In the main exhibition room.
　　(B) In the Stefan Room.
　　(C) In the Exhibitors hall.
　　(D) **In the hotel atrium.**

【解答】(D)

【解説】「Fashion Show, conducted by Nancy Smith, 5:30-8:00 p.m., Hotel Atrium.」とあるのでファッションショーはホテルのアトリウムで開催されることが分かる．

【訳】
15. ファッションショーはどこで開催されますか．
　　(A) 大展示室
　　(B) ステファンルーム
　　(C) 展示者ホール
　　(D) ホテルのアトリウム

Questions 16 and 17 refer to the following texts.

WELCOME TO UNION STREET STATIONERY
HOME　　PRODUCTS　　PLACE ORDER　　FEEDBACK

Contact Information

Customer service representatives are available to help you by telephone from Monday to Friday, 8 A.M. to 6 P.M.

Phone: 0845 555 0102

Phone: (outside UK): +44 (0) 131 555 1001

Email: service@unionstreetstationery.com

(Our representatives respond to most inquiries within 48 hours.)

Mailing address: Union Street Stationery, Concordia 21, South Street Portstyle Brighton BN40 1DH

Shipping

Product orders are usually shipped within three business days. However, specially designed products require a processing time of seven to ten business days prior to shipping. Shipping from our supply center in Edinburgh takes two to four days. Orders shipped to overseas destinations usually arrive in two to three weeks.

【訳例】

ユニオンストリート文具店へようこそ

ホームページ　　製品　　場所　　ご注文　　フィードバック

お問い合わせ

顧客サービス担当者が，月曜日から金曜日の午前8時から午後6時まで，お電話でご用件を伺っております。

電話 ― 0845 555 0102

電話（英国外から）― +44 (0) 131 555 1001

Eメール ― customerservice@unioncrossstationery.com

（お問い合わせには，担当者から通常48時間以内に返信いたします．）

住所

ユニオンストリート文具店 Concordia Road 119番地 Edinburgh EH1 2LN

配送

規格品のご注文は，通常3営業日以内に発送いたします．特別デザインの製品のご注文には，加工処理のため発送まで7～10営業日いただいております．エジンバラにある当社の供給センターからの配送は2～4日かかります．海外への配送は到着まで通常2～4週間かかります．

16. For whom is the information provided?

   (A) **Customers ordering products.**

   (B) Employees responding to requests.

   (C) Mail workers sending packages.

   (D) Company printing stationery.

【解答】(A)

【解説】誰に対して情報提供しているのかの質問．製品を注文した顧客に対する説明文である．

【訳】

16. 誰に対して情報が提供されていますか．

   (A) 製品を注文した顧客

   (B) 要求に応える従業員

   (C) 荷物配達郵便局員

   (D) 文房具を印刷する企業

17. What is described on the Web page?

   (A) Custom orders are not accepted.

   (B) E-mail inquiries are not recommended.

   (C) **International orders are available.**

   (D) All products are shipped within two days.

【解答】(C)

【解説】ウェブサイトに何が書かれているのかという質問．海外からの注文も受け付けると述べている．

【訳】

17. ウェブサイトでは何を述べられていますか．

   (A) カスタム注文は受付できない．

   (B) メールでの問い合わせを推奨していない．

   (C) 海外からも注文が可能である．

   (D) 全製品は2日以内に配送される．

Test 2　テスト2（問題数20題）

Listening test

Part 1

　Directions: For each question, you will hear four statements about a photo in your test book. After listening to the statements, please select the one that best describes what you see in the photo.

1. Look at picture number 1 in your test book.

【訳】

リスニングテスト

パート 1

　指示：写真について 4 つの説明が聞こえます．その説明を聞き，写真を最もよく記述しているアルファベット選択しなさい．

　写真 1 を見なさい．

（A）Cars are pulling into the driveway.
（B）Cars are parked in a line.
（C）Cars are parked along the road.
（D）**The skyscrapers are of various shapes.**

【解答】（D）

【解説】写真を見て高層ビルがどういう形をしているかを見る．車だけではなく全体的に写真を見るようにすること．

【訳】
（A）車が車道に入っている．
（B）車は一列に駐車している．
（C）車は道路沿いに駐車している．
（D）高層ビルは様々な形をしている．

Part 2

　Directions: You will hear a statement or question and three answers in English. They are printed on your test book and will be played once. Please select the best answer to the statement or question.

【訳】

パート 2

指示：説明または質問とそれに対する回答例が 3 件英語で一度だけ話されます．回答として最も適切なものを選択しなさい．

2. Where is the seminar being held?

　（A） **In the hall.**

　（B） On October 10th.

　（C） On business strategies.

【解答】（A）

【解説】セミナーが開催されている場所を訪ねているから，場所を答えることが必要．

【訳】

2. セミナーはどこで開催されていますか．

　（A） ホール内

　（B） 10 月 10 日

　（C） ビジネス戦略について

3. Why's the cafeteria closed?

　（A） Down that street.

　（B） Around ten o'clock at night.

　（C） **It's being renovated.**

【解答】（C）

【解説】喫茶店が閉まっている理由を尋ねている．改装中だから閉店しているのである．

【訳】

3. 喫茶店はなぜ閉店しているのですか．

　（A） その通りを下ったところ

　（B） 夜 10 時頃

　（C） 改装中

Part 3

　Directions: You will hear conversations between two or more people. You will be asked three questions about what the speakers discuss in each conversation. Please select the best answer to each question. The conversations are not printed in your test sheet and are played once.

　Questions 4 through 6 are related to the following conversation:

【訳】

パート 3

指示：複数の人による会話が聞こえます．話題について3つ質問されます．各質問に最も適した答えを選択してください．会話はテスト用紙には印刷されず，一度だけ再生されます．

次の会話に関連する4〜6の質問に答えなさい．

A: Have you two heard about the plan to enlarge the office room?
B: I heard! It's incredible! This room here is too small to work in comfortably.
C: I wonder which division will move to the larger room when construction is finished.
B: I heard the sales division will go there.
A: Ah, because it has the largest number of people in this company.
B: Maybe. I want to go to the larger room though.
C: Certainly. The company must have good money if they are willing to expand the office room.
A: I agree..

4. What is the conversation mainly about?
   (A) **An enlargement of office room.**
   (B) A change of company owner.
   (C) A decrease in employees.
   (D) An entry into a new market.

【解答】（A）
【解説】社内スペースを拡張する会話であると冒頭のAの話から理解できる．
【訳】
4. 会話は主に何についてですか．
   (A) 社内スペースの拡張
   (B) 経営者の変更
   (C) 従業員数の減少
   (D) 新規市場への参入．

5. Why does the second person say, "It's incredible!"?
   (A) She strongly opposes the news.
   (B) She wants to explain the news.
   (C) She is disappointed.
   (D) **She is happily surprised.**

【解答】（D）
【解説】Bは狭いのが当たり前と思ってきたので，にわかに社内拡張の話が出て「信じられない」と言いながら非常に喜んでいるのである．

【訳】

5. 2番に話した女性が「信じられない」と言うのはなぜですか．

(A) このニュースに強く反対しているから．

(B) そのニュースを説明したいから．

(C) 失望しているから．

(D) 非常に喜びながらも驚いているから．

6. What do the speakers imply about the company?

(A) It has an old building.

(B) It is planning to add salaries.

(C) **It is in a good financial situation.**

(D) It has many offices in the country.

【解答】(C)

【解説】会社は「The company must have good money」，すなわち儲かっているのだと話している．高水準の利益を計上している場合，会話ではこういった表現をする．

【訳】

6. 会話している人達は会社について暗に何を示していますか．

(A) 古い建物を所有している．

(B) 給与を上げる計画を立てている．

(C) 会社の財政状況は良好である．

(D) 会社は全国に多くのオフィスを所有している．

Part 4

Directions: You will listen to a single person speaking. You will be asked three questions about what the speaker says. Please select the best answer to each question. The dialogue is not printed in your test sheet and will only be played once.

Questions 7 through 9 concern the following text:

【訳】

パート4

指示：一人が話します．その内容について3つ質問が出されます．各質問に対する最も適切な回答を選択してください．話の内容はテスト用紙には印刷されず，一度だけしか再生されません．

次の文章に関する質問7〜9に答えなさい．

Come to Freund Bakery this weekend for our monthly sale!

This Saturday and Sunday, we're taking thirty percent off all our bakery products to thank our regular customers. The discount applies even to the Freund Bakery's drinks served in our tea room. You'll be sure to find your favorite bread or natural juice at a price that can't be beat. Healthy Bakery Journal says that graham bread is this season's most popular — why don't you come and try it out! Please remember, our sale ends on Sunday. Come while it lasts!

【訳例】

フロインド・ベーカリーでは，今週末に月例のセールを開催します！

日頃のご愛顧に感謝し，週の土日は，全ベーカリー製品が3割引きとなります．当店のティールームで販売している飲料も割引いたします．お好みのパンや天然ジュースをお値打ち価格でご購入できます．『ヘルシー・ベーカリー・ジャーナル』によると，全粒粉パンは今シーズンで最も人気がある商品です．どうぞお試しください．セールは日曜日までです．土日のセール期間中は，どうぞフロインド・ベーカリーにお越しください．

7. What type of products does the shop sell?
   (A) Jewelry and cosmetics.
   (B) Fruits and vegetables.
   (C) Stationary and clothes.
   (D) Baked goods and drinks.

【解答】(D)

【解説】フロインド・ベーカリーは「favorite bread or natural juice」とあるように，パンを焼き，飲料を提供している店であることが分かる．

【訳】

7. 店はどのような種類の商品を販売していますか．
   (A) 宝石類や化粧品
   (B) 果物や野菜
   (C) 文房具や衣類
   (D) 焼き上げた物や飲み物

8. What did product journal say about Freund Bakery's products?
   (A) The graham bread is the most popular product.
   (B) They are more affordable than products found at similar bakeries.
   (C) They are very popular this season.
   (D) They are made from natural ingredients.

【解答】(A)

【解説】フロインド・ベーカリーでは「graham bread is this season's most popular」と言っている．

【訳】

8. ジャーナル誌はフロインド・ベーカリーの製品について何と言っていますか．
   (A) 全粒パンは最も人気がある．

（B）他の同様のパン屋で見られる品よりも簡単に手に入る．

（C）今シーズンはとても人気がある．

（D）天然成分から作られている．

9. When does the promotion end?

 （A）On Friday.

 （B）On Saturday.

 （C）On Sunday.

 （D）On Monday.

【解答】（C）

【解説】「our sale ends on Sunday」と言っているので日曜日．

【訳】

9. プロモーションはいつ終了するのですか？

 （A）金曜日

 （B）土曜日

 （C）日曜日

 （D）月曜日

This is end of the listening test.

Part 5

Directions: A word or phrase is missing in each sentence. Select the best answer to complete the sentence.

【訳】

パート5

指示：各文で抜けている単語または語句の答えを選択し，文を完成させなさい．

10. The preparation of the materials must **be completed** by the end of this week at any cost.

 （A）complete

 （B）been completed

 （C）being completed

 （D）be completed

【解答】（D）

【解説】主語が The preparation と，ものになっていることから受け身である事がわかる．したがって「助動詞＋be＋過去分詞」になるので，（D）be completed が入る．

【訳】

資料の準備は，今週末までになんとしてでも終わらせなければなりません．

(A) 原形

(B) 完了形の受け身

(C) 進行形の受け身

(D) 受け身

11. Bill Johnson needs to **revise** the report by the end of this month. Other managers will expect his punctuality.

(A) have revised

(B) been revised

(C) being revised

(D) revise

【解答】(D)

【解説】主語が Bill Johnson である事から能動態であることがわかる．そして，(A) の「～する必要があったのに」も入れることはできるが，後半の文が未来形であることから (D) revise が入る．

【訳】

Bill Johnson は今月末までに報告書を改訂する必要があります．他の部長たちも彼の業績を期待しています．

(A) 助動詞による過去の後悔の念を表す表現

(B) 受け身

(C) 進行形の受け身

(D) 原形

Part 6

Directions: Read the following texts. A sentence, phrase or word is missing in each text. Select the best answer to complete the sentence.

Questions 12-13 refer to the following notice.

【訳】

パート 6

指示：次の文章を読んでください．問題文の文，フレーズ，単語が抜けている箇所があります．最も適切な答えを選択し，文章を完成させてください．

以下の質問 12 と 13 に答えなさい．

February 25
Ms. Jeng Fu
200 Queen Street
Kingston, ON 01123

Dear Ms. Fu:

We appreciate for your order. **12. Although** we have already shipped most of your items, the Desktop Computer（LAN 025）is currently out of stock. We are contacting our suppliers regarding your order, but the product is not likely to be available for a few days. We would be happy to substitute a similar item of your selection, or we can **13. refund** your payment for this product.

We are sorry for the inconvenience. Please contact our order department at 77-1603-3901 for further information.

Love White
Manager, Green Electronics, Inc.

【訳例】
次の手紙に関するものです．

2月25日
Jeng Fu　様
Queen Street　200番地
Kingston, ON　01123

Fu 様
　ご注文をちょうだいし．感謝を申し上げます．お品物のほとんどを既に発送させて頂いてはおりますが，デスクトップコンピュータ(型番 LAN 025)は現在のところ，在庫が切れております．お客様のご注文にご対応できますように 仕入業者と連絡は取り合ってはおりますが，まだ何日かはお時間がかかるもようでございます．代わりのお品をご選択いただくか，または本製品について代金のお戻しについて承ります．
　ご不便をおかけしてしまい大変申し訳ございません．より詳しい情報は．発注部 77-1603-3901 までご連絡くださいませ．

Love White
Green Electronics　会社　部長

12.

(A) Despite

(B) And

(C) However

(D) Although

【解答】(D)

【解説】文意より「お品物のほとんどを既に発送させて頂いてはおりますが」と，逆接の意味になるのと，「文」なので，接続詞の (D) Although「〜だが・けれども」が入る．(A) の Despite は in spite of の書き換えにもなるが，後ろは句が入る．(C) の however は文中に入ることが多い．

【訳】

12.

(A) 〜にもかかわらず

(B) そして

(C) しかしながら（文中で用いる）

(D) 〜だが・けれども

13.

(A) have been refunding

(B) refund

(C) have refunded

(D) be refunded

【解答】(B)

【解説】文意より「本製品について代金のお戻しについて承ります」となることから，助動詞 can の後は原形が入る．したがって (B) refund「返金する」が入る．

【訳】

13.

(A) 現在完了進行形

(B) 原形

(C) 現在完了形

(D) 受動態

Part 7

Directions: You will read a selection of texts, including e-mails, magazine and newspaper articles, and advertisement messages. Several questions follow the texts. Please select the best answer to each question.

Questions 14 through 15 refer to the following texts.

【訳】

パート7

指示:電子メール,雑誌や新聞記事,広告メッセージなどから出題する文章です.その文章に対する複数の質問の最も適切な答えを選択してください.

以下の14〜15の質問に答えなさい.

Peachtree Press
111 Peachtree Street NE
Suite 400 – West Building
Atlanta, GA 30303
www.peachtreepress.com
September 25

Mr. John Thomas, 1999 SW 5th Ave #100, Portland, OR 97204
Dear Mr. Thomas:

We at Peachtree Press are pleased that you have accepted to work with us again on an update and additional printing of your book "Global Tour: A Tourist's Guide." Rest assured that we understand the ongoing dramatic transformation in our field and are very glad that we can renew your previous contract with us to understand such a paradigm shift.

-(1)- Since the original "Global Tour" received such a good reception in the target markets, we would like to make sure the renewed version meets the needs of both existing and new readers. The new version will also be published in the form of an electronic book so it can be more easily distributed and bring in various potential audiences. -(2)- All provisions of the previous contract will remain unchanged, except for the renewal of your royalty fees as we consulted with you prior.

-(3)- The renewed agreement is enclosed. If you agree to it, please sign with your full name and date it. I appreciate it if you could return it to us by October 10. -(4)-

Thank you for attending to this matter in a timely manner and your wonderful contributions to the world of travel books. We respect our authors and are especially honored to work with you. Please do not hesitate to let us know if you have any questions.

Sincerely,
Catherine Carpenter
Director, Peachtree Press

【訳例】

Peachtree Press

111 Peachtree Street NE

Suite 400 – West Building

Atlanta, GA 30303

www.peachtreepress.com

9月25日

ジョン・トーマス様

住所 1999 SW 5th Ave #100, Portland, OR 97204

拝啓

ピーチツリー・プレスは，トーマス様の書籍「グローバルツアー：ツーリストガイド」の改訂と重版に関し，当社が再びご協力できることについて合意に達したことを光栄に存じ上げます．当社は業界において進行中の劇的な変化を理解しており，このようなパラダイムシフトを理解するために当社と前回の契約を更新させていただけることに大変喜んでおります．-(1)- 初版「グローバルツアー」がターゲットとする市場で好評でしたので，更新版が既存の読者と新しい読者の両方のニーズを満たすと確信しております．新版は電子書籍の形式でも出版されますので，より容易に配信できさまざまな潜在的読者を取り込むことができます．-(2)- 前回の契約の全条項は以前にトーマス様と協議したロイヤルティの更新を除き，変更いたしません．

-(3)- 更新した契約書を同封いたします．同意くださればご署名くださり日付をご記入ください．10月10日までに返送くださいますと幸いです．-(4)-

適時にご契約更新くださり，トーマス様の世界旅行に関する書籍出版のお仕事に関わらせていただくことにも感謝しております．当社が手掛ける書籍の著者の方々を大変尊敬しており，中でもトーマス様とお仕事をさせていただくことを光栄に存じております．ご不明な点がおありでしたら，ご遠慮なくお問い合わせください．

敬具，

ピーチツリー・プレス

取締役

キャサリン・カーペンター

14. Why did Ms. Carpenter send the letter to Mr. Thomas?

　(A) To ask him to review a book.

　(B) To inquire about a travel schedule.

(C) To examine that he can sign books.

(D) **To explain a modification to an agreement.**

【解答】(D)

【解説】契約更新について第 2 文で述べている．

【訳】

14. カーペンター氏はなぜトーマス氏に手紙を送ったのですか．

(A) トーマス氏に本のレビューを依頼するから．

(B) 旅行日程について問い合わせるから．

(C) トーマス氏が本に署名できるかどうか尋ねるため．

(D) 契約の変更を説明するため．

15. The wording "attending to" in line 1, paragraph 3, is closest in meaning to

(A) planning to go to

(B) discovering of

(C) **taking care of**

(D) being present at

【解答】(C)

【解説】契約更新について出版社は，何度も礼を述べていることからトーマス氏が「契約更新をしてくれた」と考えていることが分かる．

【訳】

15. 第 1 項．第 3 パラグラフの「attending to」という言葉は．

(A) 〜に行くことを計画する

(B) 発見する

(C) 世話する

(D) が存在する

16. What did Ms. Carpenter send with the letter?

(A) **A revised contract.**

(B) A writer information.

(C) A copy of a book.

(D) A book review.

【解答】(A)

【解説】「The renewed agreement is enclosed.」「更新した契約書を同封している」と述べていることから更新した契約書を送っている

【訳】
16. Carpenter 氏は手紙で何を送ったのですか？
  (A) 更新された契約書
  (B) 作家情報
  (C) 書籍一冊
  (D) 書評

17. In which of the positions (1), (2), (3), and (4) does the following sentence belong?
  "A new chapter about traveling in Southeast Asia will be sure to attract new attention."
  (A) (1)
  (B) (2)
  (C) (3)
  (D) (4)

【解答】(B)

【解説】新版は電子書籍の形式で出版し，読者層を広げることを直前で述べているので (2) に挿入するのが適当である．

【訳】
17. (1), (2), (3), (4) のうち，次の文はどこに入りますか．
  「東南アジア旅行についての新しい章は新たに注目を集めるでしょう．」

以下の質問 18 ～ 20 に答えなさい．

MEMO

Date: December 15

We would like to inform you of William Stock's upcoming retirement. Mr. Stock started his 40-year career at the Earth Fund as a wildlife forest ranger in the Louisiana Wildlife Park. He has had five different positions, finally becoming the general director of conservation for all Louisiana Wildlife Parks. He has had this position for 10 years, leading with vision and commitment. Now at 65 years old, he is leaving us for retirement.

The Board of Directors has decided to send him a Lifetime Achievement Award with a commemorative medal at the staff meeting next Monday. Following the staff meeting, we will invite all employees to attend a party to honor Mr. Stock and his great contributions. If you want to write a goodbye to Mr. Stock, please come by Anthony Brown's office to write in the book that will be presented to him at the party.

【訳例】

覚書

日付：12 月 15 日

ウィリアム・ストック氏の退職予定についてお知らせ致します．ストック氏はルイジアナ野生動物公園の野生生物森林監視員として「アース・ファンド」での40年間のキャリアを開始しました．同氏は5つの役職に就き，最終的にルイジアナ野生動物公園の保全総責任者になりました．同氏はこの役職に10年間就き，本公園のビジョンとコミットメントを先導してきました．65歳の現在，同氏は定年退職で職場を去ろうとしています．取締役会は来週月曜日の職員会議で記念メダルとともに生涯功労賞を送ることを決定しました．職員会議後，ストック氏と同氏の偉大な貢献に敬意を表して開催するパーティーにすべての従業員の皆さんを招待します．ストック氏に別れの挨拶を書きたい人がいれば，アンソニー・ブラウンのオフィスに来て，パーティーで同氏に贈る本に書いてください．

18. In what field is Mr. Stock engaged in?

　（A）Senior education.

　（B）Archiving history.

　（C）Nature protection.

　（D）City development.

【解答】（C）

【解説】「finally becoming the general director of conservation for all Louisiana Wildlife Parks（最終的にルイジアナ野生動物公園の保全総責任者になりました）」とあることから自然保護の分野に進んでいることが分かる．

【訳】

18. ストック氏はどの分野の仕事に従事していますか．

　（A）高等教育

　（B）歴史の記録保管

　（C）自然保護

　（D）都市開発

19. What will NOT be given to honor Mr. Stock?

　（A）A medal.

　（B）An award.

　（C）A book.

　（D）A photo album.

【解答】（D）

【解説】「来週月曜日の職員会議で記念メダルとともに生涯功労賞を」送られる予定で，「パーティーで同氏に贈る本」には挨拶を書くことを呼び抱えている．メダルと賞，本は掲載されているが，アルバムはない．

【訳】
19. ストック氏の栄誉を称えるために与えられないものは何ですか．
   (A) メダル
   (B) 賞
   (C) 本
   (D) アルバム

20. For how many years has Mr. Stock worked at the Earth Fund?
   (A) 10.
   (B) 15.
   (C) 40.
   (D) 65.

【解答】(C)

【解説】「Mr. Stock started his 40-year career at the Earth Fund」とあり，アース・ファンドで40年のキャリアがあることがわかる．

【訳】
20. ストック氏はアース・ファンドで何年働いていますか．
   (A) 10
   (B) 15
   (C) 40
   (D) 65

付録　お役立ちサイト

オンライン辞書
　　　http://ejje.weblio.jp/（Weblio 英和和英辞典）
　　　http://www.alc.co.jp/（アルク英辞郎 on the Web）
　　　http://www.merriam-webster.com/（Merriam-Webster）

検索（日本語）
　　　https://www.google.co.jp
コンコーダンス（文字列で検索するサイト：英語）
　　　http://www.webcorp.org.uk/
みんなの知識　ちょっと便利帳（日本語）
　　　http://www.benricho.org/

アメリカのことがわかるホームページ

アメリカ早分かり（アメリカ大使館が提供するアメリカに関する公式情報）
　　　http://aboutusa.japan.usembassy.gov/
アメリカの地図と主要都市観光情報
　　　http://www.usatourist.com/japanese/
アメリカ大統領選結果
　　　http://www.uselectionatlas.org/RESULTS/
アメリカ大統領選アトラス
　　　http://uselectionatlas.org/
アメリカ電子図書館
　　　http://elibraryusa.state.gov/

日米関係資料・ジャーナルのホームページ

外交安全保障政策に関する史料（堂場文書）
　　　http://kw.maruzen.co.jp/ln/mc/mc_doc/doba.pdf
同志社大学アメリカ研究所
　　　http://www.america-kenkyusho.doshisha.ac.jp/overview/overview.html
American Diplomacy
　　　http://www.unc.edu/depts/diplomat/
ハーバード大学ジャーナル（Harvard Asia Pacific Review）

http://www.hcs.harvard.edu/~hapr/index.html

アメリカ在外機関

US Embassy（アメリカ大使館）
  http://japanese.japan.usembassy.gov/index.html
USPACOM（米太平洋軍司令部）
  http://www.pacom.mil/
USFJ（在日米軍）
  http://www.usfj.mil/

参 考 文 献

国立国会図書館「レファレンス事例詳細」『国立国会図書館』（http://crd.ndl.go.jp/reference/modules/d3ndlcrdentry/index.php?page=ref_view&id=1000115507）

是川夕，岩澤美帆「増え続ける米国人口とその要因：人種・エスニシティ・宗教における多様性」『内閣府経済社会総合研究所』（2009）（http://www.esri.go.jp/jp/archive/e_dis/e_dis226/e_dis226.pdf）

ジェトロ「米国市場調査レポート」『ジェトロ』（https://www.jetro.go.jp/ext_images/jfile/report/07001419/1.pdf）

■ 著者プロフィール

佐藤晶子　（さとう　あきこ）
　　現　　職：近畿大学経営学部非常勤講師（英語）
　　　　　　　関西大学政策創造学部非常勤講師（社会科学入門）
　　　　　　　大阪大学招聘研究員
　　最終学歴：大阪大学大学院言語文化研究科博士後期課程単位取得退学
　　学　　位：修士（言語文化学）
　　主　　著：
　　（単著）『ボイス・オブ・アメリカ（VOA）ニュースで学ぶ英語　レベル1』（大学教育出版，2014年）
　　（共著）杉田米行編『第二次世界大戦の遺産 ― アメリカ合衆国』（大学教育出版，2015年）
　　（共著）"Public Health in Occupied Japan Transformed by SQC," *Modern Japan: Social Commentary on State and Society*, edited by Yoneyuki Sugita（Springer, 2016）

山西敏博　（やまにし　としひろ）
　　現　　職：公立鳥取環境大学　教授（言語社会学・英語教育学・認知心理学）
　　最終学歴：大阪大学大学院言語文化研究科　博士後期課程
　　学　　位：Master of Arts（Education）
　　主　　著：
　　（単著）「道産子が歩く」（静山社，1990）
　　（監修）「今こそ！『童謡』で　こころ　をなごませよう！― オトナの方のための【童謡メンタルセラピー】」―（音楽之友社，2017）
　　（共著）杉田米行編　「トータル・イングリッシュ」（大阪大学出版会，2009）
　　　　　　山西敏博，杉田米行著「15週間で英語力倍増」（大学教育出版，2014）
　　　　　　日本NIE学会編「情報読解力を育てるNIEハンドブック」（明治図書，2008）
　　　　　　小西友七・南出康世編「GENIUS　英和大辞典」（大修館書店，2001）　他多数

竹林修一　（たけばやし　しゅういち）
　　現　　職：同志社大学グローバル地域文化学部嘱託講師（英語，アメリカ文化）
　　　　　　　神戸大学大学院経済学研究科非常勤講師（英語，アメリカ史）
　　　　　　　関西外国語大学外国語学部非常勤講師（アメリカ史）
　　最終学歴：ミシガン州立大学大学院アメリカ研究科博士課程
　　学　　位：Ph.D.（American Studies）
　　主　　著：
　　（単著）「カウンターカルチャーのアメリカ　希望と失望の1960年代」（大学教育出版，2014年）
　　（単著）「実践看護英語」（英宝社，2014年）

奈須　健　（なす　けん）
　　現　　職：近畿大学経営学部非常勤講師（英語）
　　　　　　　神戸学院大学学際教育機構非常勤講師（英語）
　　最終学歴：大阪大学大学院言語文化研究科博士後期課程単位取得退学
　　学　　位：修士（国際公共政策）
　　主　　著：
　　（共著）杉田米行編『第二次世界大戦の遺産 ― アメリカ合衆国』（大学教育出版，2015年）
　　（共訳）杉田米行編『アメリカ社会への多面的アプローチ』（大学教育出版，2005年）

■監　修

杉田米行（すぎた　よねゆき）
　　　現　　職：大阪大学言語文化研究科教授
　　　主　　著
（一般書　共著）山西敏博・杉田米行『15週間で英語力倍増』（大学教育出版，2014年5月）
（一般書　単著）杉田米行編『英語で知るアメリカ ― 8つのテーマで超大国の実情に迫る ― 』（大学教育出版，2013年10月）
（ESL）杉田米行『英検®合格！ENGLISH forFUN! 小学生の2級テキスト＆問題集』（東京：一ツ橋書店，10/2016）144p

英文校正
Elisha Sum　米国編集者，ライター，翻訳者

語学シリーズ第4巻
ボイス・オブ・アメリカ（VOA）ニュースで学ぶ英語　レベル2

2017年4月20日　初版第1刷発行

■監　　修 ―― 杉田米行
■著　　者 ―― 佐藤晶子・山西敏博・竹林修一・奈須　健
■発行者 ―― 佐藤　守
■発行所 ―― 株式会社　大学教育出版
　　　　　　〒700-0953　岡山市南区西市855-4
　　　　　　電話（086）244-1268　FAX（086）246-0294
■印刷製本 ―― モリモト印刷㈱

© Akiko Sato, Toshihiro Yamanishi, Shuich Takebayash, Ken Nasu 2017, Printed in Japan
検印省略　　落丁・乱丁本はお取り替えいたします。
本書のコピー・スキャン・デジタル化等の無断複製は著作権法上での例外を除き禁じられています。本書を代行業者等の第三者に依頼してスキャンやデジタル化することは、たとえ個人や家庭内での利用でも著作権法違反です。
ISBN978－4－86429－451－5